"A. D. Thomason has been my friend for nearly twenty years. He is a learned creative who takes culture and scholarship seriously. *Permission to Be Black* is for the culture, and it's a bold message we've needed for a long time. Rooted in Christ's truth and in hip-hop's honesty, A. D. reveals why we, as Black people, must embrace our pain and vulnerability in order to find the healing and courage that we need—and that only God can supply. I highly recommend this book. But this is much more than a book recommendation; for me *Permission to Be Black* is a must-have life guide for all."
Lecrae, songwriter and recording artist

"A. D.'s voice and leadership is the very thing we've been waiting for!"
Propaganda, poet and political activist

"Whiteness has wreaked havoc on the lives of Black men with its violence and overall dehumanization. In *Permission to Be Black*, A. D. Thomason, with intimacy and vulnerability, pulls back the veil on this destruction and shows how Jesus makes a way to live in the fullness of life despite the trauma inflicted. I'm just a mediocre middle-class white guy, but I needed this message of Christ-centered transformation."
Shane Blackshear, host of the Seminary Dropout podcast

D1512313

PERMISSION
TO BE
BLACK

MY JOURNEY WITH
JAY-Z AND JESUS

A. D. "LUMKILE" THOMASON

An imprint of InterVarsity Press
Downers Grove, Illinois

InterVarsity Press
P.O. Box 1400, Downers Grove, IL 60515-1426
ivpress.com
email@ivpress.com

InterVarsity Press® is the book-publishing division of InterVarsity Christian Fellowship/USA®, a
movement of students and faculty active on campus at hundreds of universities, colleges, and schools
of nursing in the United States of America, and a member movement of the International Fellowship
of Evangelical Students. For information about local and regional activities, visit intervarsity.org.

Scripture quotations, unless otherwise noted, are from The Holy Bible, English Standard Version,
copyright © 2001 by Crossway Bibles, a division of Good News Publishers. Used by permission.
All rights reserved.

While any stories in this book are true, some names and identifying information may have been
changed to protect the privacy of individuals.

Published in association with the literary agent Don Gates of The Gates Group,
www.the-gates-group.com.

Author photos by Jaylon Ashaun
Cover design and image composite: David Fassett
Interior design: Daniel van Loon
Images: author photo by Jaylon Ashaun
          gold foil background: © Katsumi Murouchi / Moment Collection / Getty Images

ISBN 978-0-8308-4727-3 (print)
ISBN 978-0-8308-4728-0 (digital)

Printed in the United States of America ♾

InterVarsity Press is committed to ecological stewardship and to the conservation of natural
resources in all our operations. This book was printed using sustainably sourced paper.

Library of Congress Cataloging-in-Publication Data

A catalog record for this book is available from the Library of Congress.

P 24 23 22 21 20 19 18 17 16 15 14 13 12 11 10 9 8 7 6 5 4 3 2 1
Y 42 41 40 39 38 37 36 35 34 33 32 31 30 29 28 27 26 25 24 23 22 21

CONTENTS

BEYOND OUR "FAMILY FEUD"

Everyone needs a chance to evolve.

JAY-Z, *DECODED*

/Heal·ing/ n. The process of making and becoming sound; to make well again; to restore to health.

M y people are in trouble, and we don't know it. We all chase after a goal that Solomon says is ever before us but that we rarely grasp. What is before us and what do we miss? The ability to be healthy. The health I'm referring to is not physical health; it's internal, mental, and soul health. What we define as Blackness is, in a lot of ways, a result of trauma. Ignorance plays a big role too, ignorant of (1) the fact that we need to be healthy, (2) the tools we need to achieve healthiness, and (3) how to get these tools. As Jay-Z explains in "Family Feud," "We are all screwed because we never had the tools."

Why did I name this book *Permission to Be Black: My Journey with Jay-Z and Jesus*? Because I want to give you some insights (some would call them "cheat codes")—the tools of mental, spiritual, and psychological liberation to release you from the pain of being screwed because you did not have the tools.

Why Jay-Z? Ha-ha, why not? On a serious note, I did not grow up as a Jay-Z fan or stan, but more a rap appreciator for what it did for my people, Black people. At a time when we needed a voice to express our emotions without violence in the '70s and beyond, pioneers DJ Kool Herc, Kool DJ Dee, and Afrika Bambaataa brought what we know as hip-hop to life. This subcultural expression spread like fire to a main stage like none could predict. My number one MC will always be André Benjamin of Outkast fame. However, as a rap appreciator, in my humble opinion I believe that Jay-Z is the greatest rapper of all time.

I found solace in a lot of his lyrics, especially the songs expressing the burden of life in concrete jungles, like "Where I'm From." On the other side of the spectrum were songs explaining why we don't have emotions, like "Song Cry." I even appreciated some of the more boastful songs indicating a need for celebration because of our pain, like "Encore." Jay-Z spoke to my cultural story. God used him to keep me and many other Black men alive until we could appreciate Yeshua (Christ) without other folks' cultural baggage.

Side note: In this book, I will use both "Jesus" and "Yeshua" as names for Christ. I call him "Yeshua" because that is his Jewish name. "Jesus," though I have no problem saying it, is an imperfect transliteration into the English language. Mary would have called him "Yeshua." So, in the words of "Coming to America," "His momma named him Clay . . . Ima call him Clay." But I digress.

Jay-Z gave words to my pains that my body knew I had but my mouth could not put into words. He spoke to places I was in, Black places, places I was ashamed to admit even after I became a follower of Christ who still needed healing. Jay-Z gave me permission to be Black when most Christian branches said the way I was created and the experiences that formed me—my Blackness—needed to be dissolved. Early on I became a closet Black man, so I read the books of Martin Luther King Jr., Frederick Douglass, Malcolm X, W. E. B. Du Bois, and Ida B. Wells. Alongside the books I listened to Jay-Z and others for affirmation. This was the affirmation that "evangelicalism" never understood or thought I needed.

EITHER THEY DON'T KNOW, OR THEY DON'T SHOW

One of the most famous lines in Black cinema is from Ice Cube's character Doughboy in 1991's *Boyz n the Hood*, when he says, "Either they don't know, don't show, or just don't care about what's going on . . ."

I saw a post on Instagram of a Black woman encouraging the Black men who are living to rewrite the popular narrative. Indeed, based on depictions of us in entertainment—our historical forced placement on American soil as seed bearers, sexual steers, and violent gladiators (slave-on-slave fights are real)—we should be extinct.

I'm not going to say this next part eloquently. I'm exhausted from others' expectations that we rewrite our supernatural stronghold past without a manual and without the freedom to express our personhood. This hurts. The undervaluing of Black men who are seeking redemption hurts. Our culture rails on those in prison, doesn't encourage those who seek to rehabilitate themselves, doesn't take history into account, and is cavalier toward those shouldering centuries' worth of these unaddressed wounds. Rogue religious groups and gangs provide stronger community, a clear hierarchy, and a more consistent and supportive affirmation for a Black male than many people realize.

Strongholds didn't start at our birth, and they certainly are not undone because of college degrees and successful careers. Let me give you some simple numbers that I hope will bring clarity to the unique situation of Black men.

According to the United States Demographics Profile of 2019, African Americans of the diaspora make up 12.6 percent (42.4 million) of America's current population of 329 million. Take the percentage of Black men, which is right at 37 percent, out of that 12.6 percent, and you get roughly 15.7 million, if you do the math according to a *New York Times* article that talks about 1.5 million missing Black men and a nearly 20 percent gap ratio of more Black women to Black men (60 to 40). Of those 15.7 million Black men, one in three (33.3 percent, or 5.2 million) can expect to go to prison, according to the Center for American Progress and American Bureau of Justice (see also Ava DuVernay's *13th*). Which means that after you account for the African American population of males in prison, there are roughly 10 million Black men in society (3.2 percent). Now let us add some real-life "filters," if you will, on this 3.2 percent from a historical account many ignore and some think has no bearing on the present.

In *The Color of Law: A Forgotten History of How Our Government Segregated America*, Richard Rothstein expounds on the intentional policy of government to create segregation between whites and Blacks:

> Until the last quarter of the twentieth century, racially explicit policies of federal, state and local governments defined where whites and African Americans should live. Today's residential segregation in the North, South, Midwest and West is not the unintended consequence of individual choices and of otherwise well-meaning law or regulation but of unhidden public policy that explicitly segregated every metropolitan area in the United States. The

policy was so systematic and forceful that its effects endure to the present time. Without our government's purposeful imposition of racial segregation, the other causes—private prejudice, white flight, real estate steering, bank redlining, income differences, and self-segregation—still would have existed but with far less opportunity of expression. Segregation by intentional government actions is not *de facto*. Rather, it is what courts call *de jure:* segregation by law and public policy.

This speaks only to residential hurdles for African Americans, which many don't realize are a violation of the Thirteenth Amendment. We haven't broached the conversation about broken homes and neighborhoods, lack of equal opportunity, high school and higher education issues, death by law enforcement, death by each other, homelessness, mental institutions, and absenteeism.

As you consider the different categories of obstacles African Americans, specifically Black men, have had to traverse in order to "make it," the 3.2 percent figure above dwindles to an anemic one percent. These are the Black men who are alive, not imprisoned, of sound mind, and have the support system, unshakable faith, and equal resources to manifest their vision of redemption in society.

While I was writing this book, four catalytic events occurred that drive home the uniqueness of Black life and the one percent: the killings of Ahmaud Arbery and Breonna Taylor; whiteness weaponized by Central Park dog walker Amy Cooper, who lied and said an innocent Black man was harassing her; and the murder of George Floyd—I can't breathe 2.0.

Many do not see or understand this reality and it is maddening. Still we are expected to carry the weight and the expectations of the entire American population. We have to live as if we have the affirmation, resources, tools, acumen, and courage of a millennium-length legacy to thrive. *We are dying off*, physically and mentally. This expectation is crushing. It has and continues to destroy us.

> **We need the soul-searching power of God's Spirit to flow through his people to value our lives or we won't make it.**

I'll say what many don't have the words, and often courage, to say. We need the soul-searching power of God's Spirit to flow through his people to value our lives or we won't make it. We, Black men and women, need the *permission to be Black*, permission never granted to us in light of America's history.

ACCESSING THE TOOLS

After I sat down with my therapist, Don, for the first time in the fall of 2017, I got up stunned. I left thinking, *I am cheating on life with the tools and wisdom that just got dropped in my lap.* I felt a kind of survivor's guilt as I received this wisdom and insight into holistic health. I knew immediately what my community needed. I also realized they had *no clue* that these things existed, I didn't either before I sat in Don's chair. I thought about my brother and sister and our upbringing, about how my mom and dad's lives could have been transformed if they'd had these tools. From that moment I began to see Don as my kingdom version of the *Boyz n the Hood* character Furious—a Yoda type guy. To me, he was *Don Furious.*

I thought my first session with Don Furious was a fluke, so I went back for a second one. Our first session may have been like a rookie batter homering his first three times at bat. There was no way Don Furious could nail it again, again, and again. However, every time I met with Don Furious, I walked away feeling overwhelmed with life and joy. But alongside the joy I also felt overwhelmed by grief because my people were being robbed. We were victims of circumstances that caused trauma, and we were living without the tools we needed for healing.

Session after session I consistently came home to my wife, Dawntoya, saying, "I feel like I am cheating on life with the wisdom and insight I get from this man."

She would look and listen with this peculiar silence and say, "Adam, it cannot be as groundbreaking as you're making it."

I would stop her mid-thought with, "No, you don't understand. It's the book of Proverbs when I sit with Don Furious. Proverbs talks about wisdom that formed the world and how God consulted wisdom (her) as a master workman. Well, what he is telling me supersedes race, culture, class, people groups, hemispheres, and any other division you can think of."

This is the Proverbs passage I had in mind:

"The LORD possessed me at the beginning of his work,
  the first of his acts of old.
Ages ago I was set up,
  at the first, before the beginning of the earth.
When there were no depths I was brought forth,
  when there were no springs abounding with water.
Before the mountains had been shaped,
  before the hills, I was brought forth,
before he had made the earth with its fields,
  or the first of the dust of the world.
When he established the heavens, I was there;
  when he drew a circle on the face of the deep,
when he made firm the skies above,
  when he established the fountains of the deep,
when he assigned to the sea its limit,
  so that the waters might not transgress his
    command,
when he marked out the foundations of the earth,

then I was beside him, like a master workman,
and I was daily his delight,
rejoicing before him always,
rejoicing in his inhabited world
and delighting in the children of man.
"And now O sons, listen to me:
blessed are those who keep my ways."
(Proverbs 8:22-32)

No lie, every time I finished a meeting with Don Furious, I felt alive and believed everyone needed this. How our heroes of old—Ida B. Wells, MLK, Malcolm, Harriet, Queen Nzinga, and others—would have lived a different life if they had the freedom to process their internal lives and feelings without using the historic Black approach of, "We just don't talk about those things." My community continues to erode because of our historic inability to talk about our problems. And again, we don't know what tools we need to fix our problem or even where to find those tools.

For my entire life I felt that freedom didn't exist for me. I had no freedom to express. I had no freedom to mourn. I had no freedom to discard the identity boxes imprisoning me and my people. Now, through Don Furious, God had given me insights—cheat codes, if you will—to redefine something I took as normal.

In case you're wondering, cheat codes are the shortcuts and secret tricks used by video gamers to gain an advantage over their competitors and advance to higher levels. In my context, they were the tools and wisdom that the privileged used to navigate through life. Now I could do the same. In that process I also redefined my Blackness. I am now living a life I never thought was possible. I now live as an African of the diaspora who knows how to fight for a life of liberation. But it's not easy. It can be exhausting, as those of us in this place are extremely rare. However, I write this book to share those insights, cheat codes, life hacks, and *tools* so my people won't be screwed. So they can fight for and experience this liberation and freedom within the few to impact the many with a healthy mind, body, soul, psychology, and spirit.

THOUGHT PRIMER

I dare not speak for all people of the African diaspora, but my Blackness needs to be redefined. I believe wisdom is insight that transcends all stories and people groups, but opinions and cultural mores do not. What I received from Don Furious is wisdom, not cultural traditions or a biased perspective. If applied, it can change anyone's life. This is God's promise.

After sitting with Don Furious, I would reflect on Blackness and the mythical "Black card." The Black card is the imaginary license we give or take away from Black folks after measuring their level of struggle to make it in the world. It's based on skin hue, neighborhood, broken family narrative, and of course their knowledge of Black cultural icons, songs, and B movies. If you don't understand the importance of *Love Jones*, why are we even friends? (Just kidding.)

I realized that, as Black folks, we have never had a resource that spoke to our mental and social healing. We have never had a resource to extinguish the attacks on our manhood and womanhood. I would argue that we have lived a life of fragmented healing. It is a life lived outside the identity of our full story. The pastor did his or her best, but Don Furious taught me that the spiritual component of people is not the totality of our humanity. There are some things you simply cannot pray away. You need others to help you heal, and this is a gift from God. God is calling us out of this myopic way of processing healing. The new way requires a cultural "quintuple consciousness" (with apologies to Du Bois). God is calling us from compartmentalization to an integrated lifestyle. People are longing for a community that embraces our narrative while demonstrating what it means to be mentally, physically, spiritually, and psychologically healthy.

> We have lived a life of fragmented healing. It is a life lived outside the identity of our full story.

In the past, when Black people have sought after this type of holistic health, they have been shunned and accused of "acting white," being sellouts, being "soft," and so on. For many Black people, pursuing holistic wellness of the mind, body, narrative, psychology, and soul has defaulted to "praying and shouting" for deliverance. Others cry for help through acts of violence and territory protection. In reality we need unconditional love, "skin time" with someone of the opposite sex (who is not looking for sex), and a therapist who understands the kingdom of heaven and its importance in the healing process.

Internalized trauma gives off a mental stench we have become accustomed to smelling. It's like the first time you smell chitlins in your grandma's kitchen. Unless you enjoy this delicacy, your first reaction is probably to wonder why anyone would cook or eat something that smells like ten men defecated into a pot of boiling water. However, after a while the smell fades because your nose has adjusted to the odor; you've become "nose-blind." I believe we as a people have become nose-blind to the horrid stench of internalized trauma, and it is time to get free.

The ability to love and be loved is possible only once someone has gone through the healing process of redemption and full restoration. Without this experience, we cannot understand internal health in its purest form. Healing gives us clarity that helps us communicate and understand how to love and be loved. What does this have to do with "the tools," a new Black card, and Jay-Z? Glad you asked.

Let's go back to Jay's song "Family Feud" and the line, "We all screwed, cause we never had the tools." When I heard this, I felt like I'd discovered the Lost City of Gold— better yet, vibranium. My people and I have been screwed for a very long time because we have never had the tools to get healing. I would even argue we didn't know they existed.

This revelation was followed by grief and excitement. I needed to get this truth—these tools—to my people who were in need, and if that meant doing it the Killmonger way, so be it. (Sorry, T'Challa!)

As I talked with Don Furious, it became evident that the legacy handed down to me was a belief that if you ignored trauma, it would go away. But strongholds don't go away. Some commonly used phrases related to this practice were: "There are some things you don't talk about," "You just endure," "You just keep moving," "Ain't nobody got time for that," or "Let go, and let God." These phrases were used to uphold a false sense of strength in Blackness. Meanwhile, our bodies internalized the pain while Satan—a real enemy—mentally beat us to a bloody pulp. How? Burying the pain was seen as strength, and it was shameful to admit you needed to talk about the depression caused by trauma. This is what we called "healing." If I didn't break the cycle, this unhealthy practice would be my legacy as well.

Black people of the African diaspora in America are walking around wounded, in pain, and in need of healing.

Why? Because while we describe our Blackness as a symbol of strength and gumption, it has become a symbol of pain and evidence that we don't know what we don't know. (We also tend to stigmatize anyone who demonstrates the slightest knowledge of the tools we need for healing.)

Why am I writing this book? We are seeing a first for the people of the African diaspora. In 2020, information and relationships are brought to our fingertips with a simple swipe and touch of the word "search." Information is no longer hidden, and the identities that have long been ascribed to the people of the African diaspora, my ancestors, are seen for the stereotypes and mental prisons they are. I am writing this book to set us free, to talk about the diverse creations we are, and to call us out of fragmented living into wholeness. Yes, God communicates these promises in his Word. Unfortunately, the misapplication of his Word—by white folks historically and Black people culturally—leaves many believing God is powerless in certain areas. It's why many of us used Jay-Z to get through life in addition to the church. Since we lack the tools to help us understand and apply the love of God to the full person, many believe God has no answers. God is not impotent. He does have all the answers. We were just schooled incorrectly, both culturally and spiritually.

Consider Daniel Patrick Moynihan's controversial 1965 report commissioned by President Lyndon B. Johnson.

Titled *The Negro Family: The Case for National Action*, the report has had far-reaching implications:

> That the Negro American has survived at all is extraordinary—a lesser people might simply have died out, as indeed others have.... But it may not be supposed that the Negro American community has not paid a fearful price for the incredible mistreatment to which it has been subjected over the past three centuries.

President Johnson responded to this report by saying, "For this, most of all, white America must accept responsibility. It flows from centuries of oppression and persecution of the Negro man. It flows from the long years of degradation and discrimination, which have attacked his dignity and assaulted his ability to produce for his family." I would add that it has assaulted his ability to emote for the ultimate health of his family.

Generational trauma is passed down. Black folks in America have been exposed to this trauma since we came over in boats, and we're still feeling it today. As the saying goes, hurt people hurt people. However, if that's so, the opposite can also be true. Healed people can heal people. Healthy people who heal from these wounds need to share the tools they used to break the cycle of trauma. Historically, most of these tools could be accessed only if you had enough money—what we called "white money" when I was growing up. But with the digitization of the world and allies rising across ethnic lines, these tools are now in our reach. Through them God is setting many of my people free.

I am writing this book to redefine Blackness and establish a new "Black card," so to speak. Carriers of this card will no longer be ashamed of admitting that past traumas have hurt them. They will embrace the truth that it is healthy to learn how to understand trauma and heal from it. Trauma isn't just war flashbacks. It's having to raise

Healed people can heal people.

your siblings because you were fatherless. It's having to raise yourself because your mother was dealing with her own crises. It's having a father who left you and your siblings at home while he roamed the streets looking for a fix. It's being neglected because you were raised by a single parent who dealt with their trauma in silence. Aside from my own experiences, I've heard countless stories like this from others.

For too long being able to provide for yourself and others in these situations has been seen as strength or a sign of health. This new card admits the pain, grieves it, and comes out of the darkness into an Eden, the first of its kind. It's why Black folks in America both listen to Jay-Z and love Jesus (Yeshua), because both speak to our pain. Jay-Z speaks to the struggle of our everyday life and pain, while Jesus speaks to the spiritual freedom from this world we will experience when we are fully with him. For too long both have seemingly had nothing to do with each other because of compartmentalized thinking. I write to bring them together.

One thing I constantly see played out in the Black experience is the "weapon" of endurance. This served my people over centuries because of their inability to deal with their pain. In a community where no one had time to tend to anyone else's pain, they internalized their traumas and didn't know how to start the journey toward health. The new day of redemption is here.

Our situation is like a person who needs to dig a well for water, but they don't have a shovel, don't know how to dig, and don't know where to dig. Not only can they not dig the well and access water; they can't teach anyone else how to do this. This book seeks to give you the right shovels, teach you how to dig, and show you where to start digging.

This book is unapologetically Black and uses cultural references to convey my journey toward holistic health, diving deep into the need for a new Black card and the health that God has intended for us. However, make no mistake: I believe many people from other racial and ethnic contexts need a new cultural card too. That includes everyone from my rural "Appalachian white" (an MLK term) and doublewide white kinfolk, my upper-class folks (because money doesn't free you from pain), my First Nation friends, my Asian kinfolk, and everyone in between. I've talked to many friends from different cultures about the boxes and cultural mores they cling to that keep them from reaching freedom, and I've read about other cultural experiences. But I know my limits. An attempt to speak directly to their experience when I haven't lived it is disingenuous.

So, for the sake of integrity, I will speak from my truth. I will talk about the false badge of the "card of Blackness." These are traits we have ascribed to our Blackness for the sake of identity. This pursuit of an identity—one that doesn't exist—is killing us. This false badge translates to the practice of not talking about wounds because we don't know how to deal with them in a healthy way. Our emotions, bodies, and minds are held captive, and we say, "This is just how it is and who I am." That's bullsh*t. This is not who you—or we—are. This is not what God has for us. As Tupac says in "Keep Ya Head Up," "Because there are too many things for you to deal with, dyin' inside but outside you're looking fearless."

Here's to inner healing that seeks to match the smiles on the outside. Here's to not being screwed, because I am going to show you the tools the real enemy—the adversary—does not want you to have. Here's to redefining Blackness and freedom.

SHOUT-OUTS

This book is inspired by the books I have read and conversations I have had with many wise counselors. First of all, my brother, who at fifteen had to take on the role of father from the time I was twelve until the moment I sat in Don's chair. Then there's Don Worcester, who is wisdom personified and always leaves me feeling like I am cheating on the game of life. Tom and Lessie Bryce, Kenny Grant, the Youngbloods, the Hafeman family, the Bowens, the Egberts, and the Stephens—you all were the families I didn't know I needed. Alex Faith for telling me to read *Sins of the Fathers: The Atlantic Slave Traders 1441-1807*, which turned my entire doctoral studies in a new direction.

Sowande' M. Mustakeem's book *Slavery at Sea: Terror, Sex, and Sickness in the Middle Passage* helped me understand the terror both Black men and women went through physically and mentally on the journey to America.

Countless books have helped me understand the generosity of God through Hebraic idioms, including Lois Tverberg's *Walking in the Dust of Rabbi Jesus*.

Matt Rosenberg is the Messianic rabbi who led me behind the veil of God's love for people and was bold enough to acknowledge there are African Jews (some of whom are connected to me genealogically).

I was also blessed to read Dr. Curt Thompson's books *Anatomy of the Soul* and *Soul of Shame*, Bessel van der Kolk's *The Body Keeps the Score*, and Dr. Caroline Leaf's work on the brain, neuroplasticity, and regeneration of the mind and body from the cellular level, all of which she views through a kingdom lens.

My wife, Dawntoya, got wounded yet remained until God woke me up to my need for new tools. By God's love and kindness through her, I have tasted the goodness of his soul.

My kids, Zipporah, Zayne-Baltimore, and Zari, showed tremendous fortitude and love for a daddy who was in pain but didn't know it at the time.

My friends (W.A.W.G.) loved me through my darkest times the best way they knew how and are getting free themselves.

My dad, Victor, is doing new things to help us have the relationship we always wanted—#newmemories. My sister-in-law, Ebonique, read and allowed me to process through many of these thoughts with her to gain the woman's perspective.

My mom, Denise, and sis, Angela: I will always esteem you as Black women, and I have the upmost respect and admiration for you no matter your faults.

To the one percent of Black men: may you continue to fight for redemption.

Finally, to the nameless who died and lived making the trek from northern Ghana to El Mina and Cape Coast Castle going through the Door of No Return so I could be here today, to those who made it through that terror of the Middle Passage and years of degradation so I could be alive today (of whom the world is not worthy)—may God bless your actions that have been grossly lost and unrecognized; may this book honor you and the Lord who kept you in a vile time.

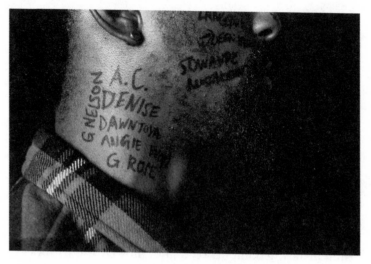

THE APPROACH

I will introduce each chapter with reflections from my journey to health and healing that I wrote down along the way. After each reflection I will expound on new tools or life hacks that were helpful for my healing process. These reflections are "cheat codes." They are the insights that left me saying, "I am cheating on life!" I want you to benefit from them as well. After these insights, the chapter will finish with a spoken-word piece designed to be a catalyst for hope. In reading reflections and insights from my healing process, I hope your own healing process can be strengthened. The title is an ethereal metaphor—not a theme—that I will keep coming back to. It is freedom time.

The new generation of Blackness is culturally variant, zealous like the Maccabees while being unashamedly proud to love Yeshua (Jesus), culture, and things that speak to our soul while not bowing down to the principalities and the power of the air and loving people of all walks of life.

I do not write this book as an expert, but I am proclaiming God does not lie; Lucifer and humankind do:

God is not a human who lies
or a mortal who changes his mind.
When he says something, he will do it;
when he makes a promise, he will fulfill it.
(Numbers 23:19 CJB)

God makes good on all his promises, and in this book I am going to show you how he did in my life and wants to in yours. He gives us permission to be fully human—physically, mentally, and spiritually. He gives us permission to be fully who he made us to be as people of the African diaspora with glorious "Black" skin. God gives us permission to be vulnerable. Permission to be whole. Permission to be Black.

INTRODUCTION

EAGLE'S WINGS

It was October 2017, and I was sitting with Don Furious for the first time. Why? I just returned from Nepal, and deep down inside I did not want to live. It had nothing to do with life's circumstances or chemical misfiring, I was tired and did not have language to express what my body was feeling. After I'd shared a chunk of my story, he caught me off-guard with, "I am surprised you are still alive."

After my shocked response, he continued, "Yeah, what you just told me of your story—and consider normal—is far from normal; it is traumatic. It is the equivalent of breaking a femur bone every day, moment by moment, for more than twenty years and expecting the body, mind, and soul to function at peak levels. The brain lights up with these traumas the same way it does when one breaks a bone. If I broke your femur every day for twenty years in various moments throughout the day, your body would eventually collapse because of the pain."

I sat there, shocked. Since I was thirteen I'd developed a kind of mantra for myself: "This does not feel normal;

this feels way off . . . but I guess I must endure." For the first time I had language to describe this feeling.

Endurance has marked my entire life. I never thought any other approach was possible. Detroit was crazy, my mom was stressed, the gangs were wild, my dad was finding himself. I hated traditional school and the social scene, and life was about enduring. I can vaguely remember some bright moments, but most of the time I lived thinking, *Just make it through this stage of life, and you'll eventually be old and die. Then you can rest in heaven.*

Even on my wedding day, endurance was on my mind. All I could think was, *Now if I can make it without doing anything stupid for fifty years, I can rest and relax. Then I am in heaven.* I was more focused on enduring marriage than celebrating it, not because my wife wasn't a gorgeous soul with a glorious form, but because all I knew was endurance.

For me, life was about enduring pain, not feeling joy— laughing about which one of us experienced the most shame and being proud about who went through the craziest situations with no help. I was trying to earn a badge awarded to those whose only consolation for en- during a messed-up life was "making it." I thought I was doing well; little did I know my body was keeping score of the physical and mental pain. My body was trying to say, "Enough!"

Don went on to say, "Adam, God has brought you this far with the only tools you knew, but those tools were not about redemption and joy. These cultural shields allowed you to make it, but God does not want us to just 'make it,' holding on to him while we traverse life. God wants us redeemed and healed, to have joy until we understand the full joy of seeing him face-to-face."

"I have no idea what that is," I replied. "I didn't know that was an option."

"I can tell. That's what your story says. But I am going to show you that it's not only an option; it's the only option God wants for us."

"I want that to be true, but I don't believe it to be true," I said. "But I trust you to be a man of wisdom, and I will follow you."

EXPERIENCING POSITIVE PAIN

Once Don asked me, "What is your ideal picture of health in the areas of marriage, kids, friendships, work, filmmaking, and creative collaboration? What do you believe God's ideal for those things is?"

I wrote down my response and reflected on it. I saw hope. This life of flourishing was in me, but I didn't want to engage the ideal because I was afraid to be let down.

"The pain of loss from joy is not the same pain that comes from abuse, manipulation, and violence. The pain of losing someone you fully loved is not the same as the pain that comes from being physically abused," Don explained.

I was stunned as he described pain in a way I'd never heard before. "To 'endure' life is to kill your emotions, to not experience negative pain," Don said. "By doing this, you also kill your ability to experience the pain that comes from living a life of joy and redemption."

CONFESSING THE HURT

We all have a healing dialect we need to uncover. The pain in our community is evidence of the absence of this language we have yet to speak. Personal reflection and conversations with Don helped me discover this reality. As I learned about trauma, internal wounds, and healing, I realized that a person can't fully express love for others if they are not healed. Based on my experience, many people living in Black communities are not mended. I would argue that this is true for other cultures as well.

We need a framework that can speak to our need for healing. We need something to help us decipher the language we know so we can figure out which road to healing we can take. I want to show you your unique expression of healing. If we are not healed, we cannot truly love or be loved because the love we give and receive will not cling to the Velcro of our souls. With nothing to cling to, it will lose the potency we expect it to have. In turn we become insatiable to please in our relationships. This is all because we're operating from a trauma deficit that leaves a pit in our heart. Others are trying to fill a cavity that formed decades before the relationship began. In a *New York Times* interview, Jay-Z reflected on how therapy helped him get in touch with the pain he was hiding. From there he was able to recognize the pain others were trying to hide:

> You don't want me to see your pain. You don't. . . . So, you put on this shell of this tough person that's really willing to fight me and possibly kill me 'cause I looked at you. . . . Knowing that and understanding that changes life completely. . . .
>
> Just realizing that, oh my goodness, these young men coming from these [streets] . . . they just in pain.
>
> You have to survive. So, you go into survival mode, and when you go into survival mode what happen? You shut down all emotions.

Those statements summed up what Don had processed with me years prior. I was amazed that Jay-Z was admitting this. What I learned from living as a Black man in Detroit is you are not allowed to say you are struggling with inner turmoil. Popular media, from rap to movies and other forms of entertainment, teach that showing pain does not get you success. In fact, it does just the opposite. It allows people to feed off you like a parasite.

> **What I learned from living as a Black man in Detroit is you are not allowed to say you are struggling with inner turmoil.**

Using coping strategies passed down from generation to generation, we've continued to display this outer strength while dying on the inside. We try to fill these pits by self-medicating through sports, accolades, drugs, sex, money, and relationships. Why? Because no one told us healthy Blackness means you can admit the hurt, get healing, and thrive. That's the insight, life hack, and cheat code. There is freedom in confession, not simply of sins, but sins done to you. These sins leave you wounded and in need of healing.

I am making a personal commitment to any person reading this who is willing to be honest and admit they need healing. I and my team from Red Revolution Ministries (iamredrev.com) will be available whether you need a voice, resources, books, or help in finding a counselor. It is that serious. I want us all to know how to speak to each other's need for healing and be willing to partner in the journey toward liberation. God's promise in Isaiah 40 speaks volumes about the journey ahead of us:

> Haven't you known, haven't you heard
> that the everlasting God, ADONAI,
> the Creator of the ends of the earth,
> does not grow tired or weary?
> His understanding cannot be fathomed.
> He invigorates the exhausted,
> he gives strength to the powerless.

Young men may grow tired and weary,
even the fittest may stumble and fall;
but those who hope in *ADONAI* will renew
    their strength,
they will soar aloft as with eagles' wings;
when they are running they won't grow weary,
when they are walking they won't get tired.
    (Isaiah 40:28-31 CJB)

The Scripture says we will "soar aloft as with eagles' wings." Here is to the start of eagle's wings.

CHAPTER 1

THE MASQUERADE

Masquerading like he's got it figured out.

In my audiobook *Confessions of an Ex-Evangelical: Why I Left Christianity and Started Practicing Jesus*, I talk about my transition from Detroit to my time at Savannah College of Art and Design (SCAD). After getting all of my stuff into my dorm room, my dad handed me a pair of socks with a pack of condoms inside and left. I was suddenly alone in a dorm room with no idea of what to do next at college in the South, let alone in life. God met me in college at age seventeen and through Brian Buck my life was changed. However, if you want the full context of my Detroit story, be sure to listen to that book because this next story picks up where that one left off.

There I was, spring of 1999, finishing up my intro classes for the semester. I walked into my last class session of Intro to Life Drawing. I was green-eyed with, as Martin Lawrence's Jerome character would say, "breath smelling like Similac." This class was supposed to be one hundred percent still objects and spheres. We already knew what our final grades would be, so I guess the professor decided to mix things up a bit. Instead of his usual process of setting up the wood objects, turning off the lights, and placing a spotlight on the subjects, he threw a curveball. I guess business as usual would be too boring—typical at an art college. Everything is art, right? Besides, he needed to prep us for drawing every inch, crack, and crevice of the human form, from twenty-eight- to eighty-year-olds. And boy did he!

I and the other students had our heads down as we casually settled in at our drawing tables, arranged in a circle around the subject to be drawn. We could hear the excitement in our professor's voice as he announced, "I have a surprise for you all!"

I'm focused on my drawing materials. I take out my pencils and drawing pad and arrange them meticulously on the desk in front of me. As my professor says, "All right, let's get started," I finally look up to see our drawing subject. It's our professor's girlfriend, taking off her clothes.

On the outside, I have a stone face as I look around the room. On the inside, I'm thinking, *Yoooo! This woman is gorgeous. Her body is amazing! But, uh, is this the norm in this culture?* I look around for social cues, like someone fidgeting or looking for their keys. Seeing no one else outwardly expressing my internal feelings, I swallow my surprise. I decide to internalize and view this women's nakedness as sacred, while committing to draw her form for class as she agreed to freely give it away.

At this time I knew nothing about the Bible. And I was a typical college freshman who had no clue what a standard was. This situation impacted my body, mind, and soul, but I did what I thought any other person would probably do in the moment. I swallowed my feelings and emotions. As Lauryn Hill observes in "Adam Lives in Theory" (from the *Unplugged* album), I was "masquerading like he got it figured out."

So I said nothing and masqueraded as if seeing her body, an exposed gift of sacredness, meant nothing. I acted as if it were not stimulating and used cliché phrases like, "How cool is it that our professor wanted to set us up for the stages in our artistic journey?" All the while, all I could think was, *Y'all we just saw a gorgeous woman nude!*

Let me pause to give you some context. I wasn't a kid who accidentally found "porno mags" under my dad's bed or was shown them by my friend Johnny (it's always a Johnny. Sorry, Johnny!). I saw slides in high school when they wanted to scare us into not having sex, and I had one friend who had a random VHS tape in high school he showed us. We laughed him to shame, and he quickly turned it off. So, until my time at SCAD, my interaction with the naked female form was limited.

That day in art class, I realized that the art world is a different culture. In this culture, the feeling of sacredness is somehow numbed. No one taught me to have reverence for the sanctity of the human body, but I sensed it on my own. For the next five years, through hundreds of nude drawing classes and experiences in the fashion world, the sacredness was indeed killed. Thank the Lord it did not send me into a spiral of porn addiction (no shame to those fighting to be free from that).

Still, it killed an innocence in me I didn't know I had. To this day I don't know which death had the most impact: losing my innocence and sacred view of the female body or losing my freedom to talk about things I tangibly felt in my body since they were contrary to the cultural and environmental norm. It became habit to internalize what I felt and thought—staying silent for the sake of remaining in the good graces of those who could make or break my professional success.

The human body itself is not sinful. We know this because God declared it good (Genesis 1:31). The problem is our interpretation of that body in different spaces and what God did after the fall in response to the coverings Adam and Eve made for themselves. In the moment God saw that Adam and Eve had covered themselves, he could have demanded they remove their clothes. He could have said they were never intended to wear clothing. However, God chose to remove their version of coverings and give them his version. Why? I believe he knew what we could never know: that after their eyes were opened, it would be impossible for men or women to see the body in its sacred pre-fall form without a skewed animal-instinct or fleshly distortion to it.

Why do I say this? Because I had to internally process my stance on and experience with this issue for most of my life. This type of internalization would be considered mild but, sadly, it's par for the course. It affects our bodies, and we need to talk about that on the road to freedom.

BLACKNESS REDEFINED

Just as in Lauryn Hill's song, I believe we all "live in theory, trying to turn stones into bread" and masquerade "like we got it figured out." There are many situations big and small we would love to process, but fear of being shamed stops us. Life without a guide is theory. Most of us are living in theory just as previous generations did, going all the way back to the Door of No

Life without a guide is theory.

Return in places like El Mina and Cape Coast Castle in Ghana and Goree Island off the coast of Senegal.

The people who stepped through those doors had no idea what was to come. They didn't know the impact of slave ships, the Middle Passage, or the "new world" that would separate them from their language, land, family, and identity. They didn't know they would be burdened with the task of proving themselves, turning stones into bread.

They didn't know the terror they would face, as Sowande'
M. Mustakeem's book *Slavery at Sea* describes:

> With young girls and adult women this invasive pro-
> cedure meant strangers' frantic groping about their
> breasts, hips, buttocks, and vaginal areas. Male cap-
> tives underwent similar public molestation to make
> certain "they have no Mark in the Groins, or Ficus's
> about the *Anus*, or Marks of Scabs having been about
> the *Scrotum*" or other orifices. Foreign trades surveyed
> slave men according to the strength their muscles
> conveyed, often reinforcing stereotypical assump-
> tions of black male sexual prowess. Knowing the vital
> assets both groups represented in the sexual economy
> of slavery, interested buyers scrutinized the lucrative
> potential that their captives' bodies could generate for
> future reproductive and breeding purposes.

My ancestors, going back to the slave trade, have known
nothing but internalizing terror heaped upon them and
the inability to process their humanity.

That day at SCAD, I learned that putting on the mask
was perceivably better than acknowledging internal
feelings for which I didn't have words. I needed to prove
myself to the culture and turn stones into bread. And I
had to do it in silence to justify my presence. If I'd spoken
up, I would have been shamed with accusations like, "You
just don't get it," or "You don't understand art."

CHEAT CODE NO. 1

Stop internalizing your pain. Drop the mask. Speak up. I believe our culture has prided itself on turning stones into bread to prove ourselves so we can belong. When it comes to Blackness, we've created standards that drive people underground into silence. They swallow their feelings and are robbed of their innate sacredness—all because of a "Black card" upholding the mantra, "There are things you just don't talk about."

Trauma backs us into a human corner where external realities lay bare our humanity. Expressing pain, feeling feelings, blushing, being uneasy—these are all signs of weakness and warrant being labeled weak, not Black. However, we are people made up of body, mind, soul, and spirit. I need to be able to say "I need you" and not get chastised as weak or—dare I say—white.

In the movie *Juice*, Tupac Shakur's character, Bishop, says during a conflict with a so-called friend, Q, "I am the one you need to be worried about . . . *pawtna!*" What if instead he'd said, "I'm tripping with this gun, I shot Steel, and I don't know what to do. Help ya boy, Q"?

Yeah, right! Instead we take the gun, we man up, and we kill anyone who challenges us, because "we got the juice and need it."

If a woman steps out of line, we check her—through verbal or physical abuse—instead of civilly saying, "Your actions hurt me."

If I am not praised enough, I knock down as many people as possible.

If I am not loved by Mom or Dad, I seek that affection from someone else instead of acknowledging the hurt.

I use anything—drugs, acclaim, degrees—to find worth and self-medicate in order to cope with the things trauma stole from me in my formative years.

Those five years at SCAD (from seventeen to twenty-two years old) served as a breeding ground for "Lucy," as Kendrick calls him. It was a time when I masqueraded like I had it figured out, and negative patterns set in.

Satan is a coward and does not care whether you have the tools. He wants to inflict pain and will use whatever he can in your environment to do so. He uses shame and internalization to keep us silent, but God did not create us to be slaves to fear, shame, or the temptation to prove ourselves and our Blackness by turning stones into bread.

For centuries we as Black folks didn't have the freedom to say we were tired. Historically there have been laws and cultural mores that fostered a sense of terror that laid the foundation for internalization. If you were exhausted during these times, you kept going. You picked cotton or the whip, castration, and sexual abuse came. There was no freedom to call out inhumane treatment. If you spoke up you were lynched. We didn't even have the freedom to eat where we wanted because our identity as humans was limited by legislation.

From the Greenwood Massacre of 1921 to Freedom Rides and Bloody Sunday, these painful facts rang true. We couldn't worship at the white man's church because we weren't welcomed or allowed. But we couldn't pray in our own churches without fear of disruption from bombs or snipers. The 2015 massacre of the Charleston Nine reminds us that this is still true today. We couldn't live in our neighborhoods without the fear of death from the hand of the white man then or the hands of our own kind now. What is normal and embedded in the Black identity is the existence of holistic terrorizing trauma.

The sacredness of life has been taken from us, and we have internalized it for too long. This has led pop-culture icon Charlemagne to speak about mental health in his book *Shook One: Anxiety Playing Tricks on Me*. Our people have not been able to process our existence as whole persons. Research confirms that unprocessed trauma impacts our brains and bodies on a cellular level. Science now shows us how trauma is passed down genetically. (For additional reading, I recommend *The Body Keeps the Score* by Bessel van der Kolk, *The Soul of Shame* by Curt Thompson, and *The Souls of Black Folk* by W. E. B. Du Bois as starting places.)

The Black man and woman have not known a time in the Americas when they were free from the possibility of imminent danger. In 2021, Black parents still have to have "the talk" with their children. Not the sex talk but instructions on the "proper" conduct to display if pulled over by the police as Maria Taylor calls it "comply or die." This is a life-or-death conversation. I have had it with my eleven-year-old daughter and eight-year-old son. There are protocols we must abide by because our lives depend on it. Other communities do not have this burden or concern.

So with a history of inability to objectively process critical levels of shock—spiritually, emotionally, physically, socially, or psychologically—how do you get a group of people to begin to open up? You start with leaders being honest about the pain and the need to mourn and heal. You start with acknowledging the times are changing. Laws have changed or are being enforced, allowing a greater ability to live into the freedoms we have as US citizens. We are able to celebrate some aspects of our humanity that our former generations—even our parents—couldn't have. Without the lenses to see this clearly, we will continue the cycles we are desperately trying to break. Meanwhile, our real enemy remains coy, as if he has nothing to do with it.

The adversary has no compassion for you personally or for us as a people (1 Peter 5:8). The way we have been groomed and reared to fight this troubled existence is to internalize our personhood. Though we are free to vocalize our pain, Satan succeeds in his attempts to convince us otherwise. He often wins, but we still must confront our pain, admit it, and live holistically. I will explain how to do this later in chapter twelve.

What was your breeding ground for silence and inter-nalized shame? In talking with Don Furious, I realized mine started when I was twelve. I didn't vocalize my feelings of rejection from constantly being compared to my two older siblings. I was the child who was not planned or "didn't get parented," so I got leftovers. I had an ab-sentee dad during the crucial window of twelve and beyond and a mother who was recovering from a horrific shooting (and two years later was further overwhelmed when my sister had a baby while still in high school). I absorbed and internalized a ton.

On top of that, there was a layer of alertness one had to have to navigate Detroit—and later the South—without a guide. It was a legacy all the generations before me had lived. So by the time I got to SCAD at seventeen, I had perfected the practice of inter-nalizing and remaining silent. This is why Don Furious said to me, at thirty-seven, "I am surprised you are still alive."

> **Performing to turn stones into bread only gets you achievements that can be snatched away from you.**

We can rediscover Blackness through transparency. What was taken from you and devoured by trauma? The ideal is gone. Eden does not exist when we come out of the womb, though we have an innocent Edenic mentality. Once we identify our breeding ground and realize through trial, error, and distress that our environment is unsafe and far from Eden, we feel the need to develop survival mechanisms such as internalization and covering up. One key to understanding the enemy's scheme is being able to understand your habitat and recognize the patterns of internalizing and shame in your own life.

No longer can we call it healthy to masquerade like we have it all figured out. Performing to turn stones into bread only gets you achievements that can be snatched away from you. The good news is that our Eden, true joy, can be birthed out of the darkness. Don Furious gave me a colossal cheat code and tool: to do the work and vocalize the pain is better than internalizing it and pretending as if it doesn't exist. You have the permission not to pretend anymore.

New Horizon (A Spoken Word)

Bread given to *breed*
Because we were bred to *breed*
Shamed to *speak*
Whips, chains, auctions, violation of the body
    and *conscience*
They sold off more than our *bodies*
Looted, suited, and *booted*
To be present with Sambo's *smile*
Meanwhile
Meanwhile

Haughty
The spirit of our *oppressor*
Our lineage only knows *stressors*
The enemy discipled us into
Being the *aggressor*
Freedom, not of this origin's *soil*
But this ain't our *soil*
No more vain *toil*
From the door of no return
With no ability to *speak*
The wind of God kept us
Despite the plan to bury us *deep*
The charade to be *over*
We get *closure*
Mourn for *then*
Mourn for *now*
Now *bow*
Bow!!!
It.will.bow.

CHAPTER 2

HELPLESS HOPE

Don't slip . . .

*/Trau·ma/ n. A deeply distressing
or disturbing experience.*

remember the first time I saw my father lift my brother off the ground, with a Thanos-like strength. Growing up, my siblings and I had a saying: "If you made Dad mad, chances are it was your fault." My dad was mild-natured; until that moment I'd never seen him fly off the handle. He was five-foot-ten on a good day with an average frame and looked like he was from a time period that didn't believe in weights. My brother, on the other hand, was six-foot-five in the eighth grade. Yes, that kid had the Batman abs. We worked out together in the basement. So the thought of him ever being "handled" never crossed my mind.

I was in the kitchen, and I saw my dad dart past me like the Flash. He hemmed up my brother, grabbed him by the neck, and pinned him against the wall. As my dad lifted my brother off the ground, I stood there, paralyzed. I thought, *Aaron, what did you do? What did you say?* I am much smaller, so there was no way I could help this dude. But I remember seeing how helpless my brother was. I saw the shock in his face and felt that, if I were endowed with the strength of Thor, my dad would have been done at that moment! But I was not Thor, and I didn't like the paralysis I felt in my gut. The inability to help my brother was tangible. I knew if I said or did anything, I would be next, and who wants to be lifted off the ground? I mean, if Thanos can handle the Hulk like that, I didn't have a chance.

I had to internalize a ton at that moment. The inability to speak up and physically come to the defense of my brother has stuck with me to this day. It made me a vocal advocate for those who experience systemic oppression through physical, mental, social, and verbal abuse. I never found out what my brother did or said, and I never saw that reaction from my dad again. I didn't want to be lifted off the ground that day, but I also thought what happened to my brother was his fault. I believed this so much that I did not say or do what I should have. I felt I should have put myself in harm's way in some way, shape, or form in order to help him.

Trauma is a deeply distressing and disturbing experience. It was obviously distressing and disturbing for a boy to see his brother being handled this way. Was there a conversation about this incident? No. Was there forgiveness asked or offered? No. Did anyone (myself included) ask my brother how he felt? No. Did my brother and I process this situation? Not until a year ago. We internalized it, swallowed the shame and pain, and "moved on." This was the Black way, right? We don't talk about things like this.

The tendency I have experienced within the Black community is to internalize the distressing and disturbing physical, sexual, and emotional abuse we or our loved ones have experienced or witnessed. Because of legislated limits on our humanity throughout American history, we must grieve the fact that what we've called normal was a traumatizing existence.

> **Because of legislated limits on our humanity, what we've called normal was a traumatizing existence.**

In "Adam Lives in Theory," Lauryn Hill tells us not to "regress or slip into hopelessness." I would love to say that did not occur in the incident between my brother and my father or other situations between my brother and both my parents, but we regressed and slipped into hopelessness. It became hopeless to speak about issues that affected us deeply. We reverted from the hope that came from viewing our house as a haven from the outside world. Instead, our haven became rooted in internalizing our emotions. Our attitude about our home life during childhood was simply to endure and jump at the first chance to move out. Our house's purpose became purely functional. It provided food and shelter. We had to look elsewhere to meet our mental, spiritual, and psychological needs.

It reminds me of the only time I felt a tangible terror. It was when I hiked Mt. Shasta. Our guide kept driving it into our heads as we walked roped together on a high-degree pitch with crampons: *don't slip*.

HISTORICAL REFLECTION

I remember the first time I read an account of what my ancestors went through during the Middle Passage, when African men and women were violently enslaved and transported across the Atlantic Ocean to the Americas. I felt the suffocating reality of having eyes wide open but being blinded by the darkness at the bottom of the boats. I felt the sweat, vomit, defecation, and other body fluids that filled the sleeping spaces and smelled their scents in the air. I felt both the horror of having to live through this and the horror of not being able to process the trauma. Imagine being among the most vulnerable. Mustakeem writes:

> Deborah Gray White argues that being both black and female, enslaved women were the most vulnerable group within antebellum slave communities.

Subjected to violating scrutiny, sold, and permanently
made a part of the global enterprise of captivity, their
lives were in a constant state of exploit and danger
not merely within plantations but beginning on the
African side of the Atlantic. "When the women and
girls are taken on board a ship, naked, trembling, ter-
rified . . . they are often exposed to the wanton
rudeness of white savages."

Mustakeem adds that the white sailors wielded "a consciousness of powerlessness and defeat" over their female
captives designed to reinforce their sexualized status.

BLACKNESS REDEFINED

The Black experience is still one that is deeply distressing
and disturbing in its reality. It is traumatic. Those traumas
include everything from body and sexual traumas to
lynching to modern-day police shootings, and the Black
community needs liberation from the constraints of the
past. We need to acknowledge and address the painful fact
that we have been targeted by society in a way that has
silenced us, paralyzed us, and prevented us from processing the holistic nature of who we are for over four
hundred years. We address it by saying, "No more," by
acknowledging that although society is not tilted in favor
of the Black community, we can live free and healed.

Holistically, the needle has moved enough to empower
us to stop the cycle of internalized trauma. The things we

have experienced historically as a people and the things that have happened to us in the present day can easily be used to justify the fact that internalizing feels like the only way of life for many of us. The problem is, it's killing us. Mental, spiritual, physical, and psychological health is a problem. This is a problem that can't be fixed in the church house on Sunday morning. It does not suffice when you consider the violence, objectification, and medication used to numb the things we saw in our homes and outside in the culture growing up.

Traumas shape us like a potter forms clay. What wounds paralyze you? What emotional injuries did you swallow and internalize? How have they shaped the way you view your family and society and how you engage with others? What wounds from your youth have ushered you into regression and nudged you into hopelessness because you know nothing else?

CHEAT CODE NO. 2

Trauma is not an accurate representation of life. In other words, the experience of negative things in life does not mean life itself is negative. Though trauma may have been a frequent occurrence in your daily life, God can always interrupt it with something new.

Don Furious gave me insight into the wisdom of God when he explained how the brain reacts to physical and emotional situations. Your neurology (the brain's belief patterns) defaults to what it thinks to be true based on situations that are repeatedly distressing or joyous. Our psychological default depends on our childhood experiences. But Don also told me, "God has engineered the body in a way that will help you reverse traumas, break free and heal from this trauma-induced default, and reset it. There is hope, Adam."

Jay-Z on his album *4:44* says, "Cry Jay-Z. . . . We know the pain is real, but you can't heal what you never reveal."

There is hope that we don't have to slip and regress into hopelessness. There is hope that our past does not predict our future. There is hope that we can talk about the traumatic things and find freedom in them. There is hope that healing comes in revealing. You have the permission to reveal and heal.

> **There is hope that our past does not predict our future.**

Am I Wet? (A Spoken Word)

The life of a fish is under water,
But we are without *gills*
Swim *nigga*,
Twerk something *b*tch*
Swim fast and don't *breathe*
You will *drown*
Told and taught to internalize the liberty

To express our most authentic self for the sake of
Survival
We have been holding our
breath underwater for centuries and
each generation is passing out from *it*
We have long passed *out*
We don't know *it*
Passed out from the lack of the ability to
     express feelings
Dead was the normal
Passed out from equating provisions to *love*
Possessions were the equation of *love*
Legally that is all we had
So, this chain ain't gaudy it says I am free
To be *loved*
YES, JAMES EARL JONES YOU DO
HAVE TO LIKE *ME*
But "liking" someone is an emotion, an expression
     that has been so foreign to our people it is like
     asking a horse to be a guard dog in a junkyard.
There is no concept in the framework for this.
No more *regression*
No more suppression of the purest *expression*
No more *hopelessness*
Release my brothers and sisters from the chokehold
     that has lifted the being of who we are off
     our *feet*

How did THAT make you *feel?*
Loved
Reveal and heal
Expression is the new *Black*

CHAPTER 3

FAUX MIRACLE

Just accept it.

/Wound/ n. A mental or emotional hurt.

Tere was a faux miracle on Detroit street that happened when I was young. It was a result of lying for the "style."

One of the biggest fights I had in my life came at ten years of age in one of the worst schools in Detroit, Michigan: Hampton Middle School. This was a school where cats threw desks at teachers (I guiltily admit I was one of them), where getting jumped and fighting was the norm, and where teachers functioned more as guards than educators. So why I did what I am about to explain to you is still confusing to this day—*to dis day.*

"Can you see that sign?" asked my mom.

"No," I replied.

"Son," she said, "we are just feet away from the billboard. Are you sure you can't see it?"

"No, Mom. I can't see it," I said as I squinted my eyes to blur my vision while we rolled down the highway.

"Then we need to go see the eye doctor to get you some glasses," she replied.

The truth was, I could see the billboard but had decided I wanted to start wearing glasses as a fashion statement. Now, why I didn't just ask my mom for glasses is beyond me. Maybe because this was before fake frames and clear prescriptions were in. Glasses did not go hand in hand with fashion and the cool hipster vibe. I had to have some frames, but to this day I cannot tell you why I wanted these joints. But I did, and I lied my way into them.

Hindsight is twenty-twenty, and I now must admit that they were the worst pair of glasses! Back then, though? I thought I was killin' 'em. I remember thinking they made me look smart, but that turned out to be counterproductive because—for one thing—I got picked on all the more for having them. So after enduring ridicule for a few months, I decided I wasn't going to wear the glasses any longer. Still, I needed to find a way to justify this to my mom, who had spent her money on those glasses.

This next line I am about to write is what they call an Easter egg in the movies. I'm writing this in 2020; as of this day, my mother still thinks God healed me of severe blindness. I *knoooooow* (insert appropriate GIF here). So, that is where the story turns.

I am thirty-nine years old, and the experience of her son having severe blindness between the ages of ten and eleven and then being healed has been a standard part of my mom's story and faith journey for twenty-seven years now. My wife has even asked me if I'm ever going to tell my mother that I never needed glasses. My response? "No. God responded to her faith in trusting him to heal. Though I wasn't healed, God was at the extension of her faith, not me."

I *knooooow!* Why haven't I told my mom?

Sometimes I think people need stories to keep them believing in the thing they have invested so much of their life in. I'm not saying it's right, but this is from a guy who will take selfies with people because they are convinced I am a football player being humble, so I stay silent and give them their story. I *knooooow!*

> **People need stories to keep them believing in the thing they have invested so much of their life in.**

HISTORICAL REFLECTION

I remember reading *The Confessions of Nat Turner* when I was a teenager. An enslaved African American preacher, Turner was described as the leader of a rebellion to free himself and others in the summer of 1831.

One of the things that stuck out to me about Turner's story was not his courage to lead an uprising but his discovery of two different Bibles. Turner discovered that there was one Bible for enslaved Blacks and a different Bible for whites. His discovery was a revelation to me as well. The slave Bible had removed all verses that spoke of liberation and God's kindness and love toward all people. Also removed were verses that talked about the golden rule, how to treat your neighbor, and God's judgment toward those who did not treat all his creation well. When Turner discovered this, he felt called to overthrow this hypocritical system.

In reflecting on Turner's story, Lauryn Hill's song "I Get Out" comes to mind. Her lyrics say, "I've just accepted what you said, keeping me among the dead." I couldn't help but think how we as a people just accepted what the white slave masters told us about God and the Bible and a "white" Jesus, only to realize none of it was true. The version of the Bible they gave us was altered. Turner realized he had been presented with a false narrative. For a long time, he and others just accepted it. This kept them imprisoned in a state of death instead of life.

BLACKNESS REDEFINED

Wounds are defined as mental or emotional hurt. For too long in the Black community we have accepted the things our culture and parents told us about the spiritual, mental, and psychological components of who we are.

Our hurt was glossed over. This caused us to view life through an unhealthy lens that presented us as healthy. So as trauma gives us distressing situations, we process our mental and emotional wounds through false lenses. The scars are attached to trauma and are compounded by recurrent trauma.

Many people have stories like mine, stories that would lead Don Furious to say, "I am surprised you are alive." We use them as a badge of honor, as if our pile of unprocessed trauma proves how strong we are. Having had the chance to work on my own issues, my heart grieves for those who are not able to express their authentic selves. Your true expression has been repressed, you have been told in many ways to just accept what was said. Through it all, your inner person is kept among the dead. Yes. This approach to life keeps us among the dead mentally and psychologically.

Through reading this book or through an eventual conversation, my mother will find out the truth that God did not heal me. However, God still performed miracles in her life because he knew she was seeking him and not the miracle itself.

God is the one we should seek. For too long we have accepted the truth of our internalized states while dying inside and placing the blame on God. Whether we knew this or not is not the full point, though. The point is we don't have to accept the false reality of putting up a front and ignoring our pain as a form of trusting God. The way we have trusted God to be with us as we processed life through wounds post-trauma is the same way we must trust him with our truest self and feelings.

Even if the trauma has stopped, the wound—the mental and emotional hurt—remains and will continue to be an issue until we name it. In the encounter with the Gerasene demoniac, Christ asks him, "What is your name?" (Mark 5:9). Many of us need to name the trauma that has wounded us. We need the freedom to process the trauma, so we can name the feelings it elicits. The feelings may range from rage to deep sadness. Many of us need to be held, walked with, and consoled with no strings attached. I believe the Lord has birthed us for this because his Word reminds us, "There is a friend who sticks closer than a brother" (Proverbs 18:24).

By processing my trauma with Don Furious, I realized that my wounds were the glasses through which I saw life. I thought that was God's best for me, and my Blackness at the time affirmed it. This was the legacy handed to my parents and their parents before them and so on, all the way back to when the first enslaved African stepped off a boat onto American soil. But Don Furious uttered these mind-blowing words: "This is not God's best for you. It is what you have known to be best, but endurance and internalization are not God's best for you."

CHEAT CODE NO. 3

A trauma that leaves an unhealed wound leads to what I call "deficit living." I define deficit living as subconsciously putting everyone in an emotional hole that they must work to climb out of by demonstrating and proving their love. But once this deficit exists, it's impossible for them to climb out of—especially if they show any sign of being connected to past traumas through unhealed wounds. You also exist in a deficit—an insatiable void that you cannot fill. It's deepened by accusations and belief that no one loves you, people always leave, or no one wants to give you their best.

With the strength of Black Panther's suit that absorbed ten thousand blows, trauma will unleash itself eventually and disintegrate everyone in its path. The thought "No one has time for me" keeps you among the dead in your subjective belief. Because the trauma is not named and the wound is not healed, you will have everyone working overtime to fill a hole that is too big to fill in this lifetime because this Grand Canyon of trauma started way before your current relationship.

With this as your reality, you cut people off emotionally and justify it because you don't know how to name traumas and hurts. Meanwhile, you're exploding—punching walls here, throwing a table there, and breaking a phone—because you believe no one knows you or understands your situation. They may not understand, but neither do you. You must stop swallowing your pain and believing the myths that you don't experience stress, nothing gets to you, and no one can hurt you. Responding in a reactive way demonstrates that things do get to you. No, it's not passion. It's unprocessed hurts. I'm writing from firsthand experience.

God made us all with the same emotions; some of us can express them more freely than others if the imperfections of the world haven't interrupted that freedom. The good news is that even if that freedom has been interrupted, God can restore the years the locusts have eaten.

> **God can restore the years the locusts have eaten.**

I see feelings and emotions as the taste buds of the soul. If God wanted us to eat food only to fulfill the function of satisfying hunger, he wouldn't have given us taste buds. Therefore, if God wanted us to live without feelings and emotions, he would have made us robots.

The lenses traumas give you are wounds, emotional and mental hurts, and you see everything through them. Understand, if these wounds are not healed, your body internalizes them and your loved ones—despite your well-intentioned motives—will pay for it because you have not learned to say the most significant three-word phrase there is: *that hurt me.* This phrase changed my marriage and friendships and continues to do so today. I had to develop the practice of saying what hurts.

CHEAT CODE NO. 4

New Blackness celebrates the freedom to name the distressing situations that created the mental wounds we accepted as normal. This old practice is "keeping us among the dead" and preventing us from expressing our most authentic selves. Let's not give the enemy a story to tell and call it "Blackness" or "trusting God." Let's name the traumas and wounds and see ourselves and our loved ones experience the abundance God has for us. The fullness of God's riches is available now, on earth as it is in heaven. You have permission to name your freedoms and have peace now.

A New Name (A Spoken Word)

What is your *name?*
Kunta . . . Kunta *Kinte*
We have maintained the life of Toby
For too *long*
Masking our internalization of hurts
For *strength*
Look, I took the worst beating of us all, and only
     one tear came down my cheek WHILE
     LOOKING AT YOU, MR. *MAN*
I just needed boots, BOOTS . . .
My name ain't Toby and those whips
Gotta *die*

Cuz it will be you or me, and I damn for sure ain't
    running no *more*
It has not been *easy*
Life had no chocolates for my people and *me*
So mourn is what we will do.
Give names to the pain that terrorized us from
    emotional *liberation*
My life is no longer among the *dead*
I don't believe you *anymore*
What is that sound you *hear?*
A new day, not a dream in the sky passing us *by*
Beulah land is *now*

CHAPTER 4

COIN DROP

Traditions kill freedom.

/E·mo·tion/ n. Instinctive or intuitive feeling as distinguished from the reasoning of knowledge.

I tried a ton of things in my pursuit to find myself. I tried my hand at playing the guitar, dude ranching, and even mountain hiking. One of the memories that still makes me laugh is the time I was determined to be a magician. It was while I was still attending SCAD. I fell in love with the idea of being a magician and bought an intro level how-to book of tricks at Barnes and Noble. The first trick on the list was the coin drop. I must have tried this trick so many times that you would have thought I was auditioning for *The X Factor*. This was before Pinterest was even a thing, but "Nailed it!" would have been the perfect description of my exaggerated evaluation of my sleight-of-hand skills.

I easily mastered card tricks, but when it came to tricks involving coins and other objects, I was a walking "Nailed it!" disaster. The idea is to give the illusion that you are making the coin disappear while grabbing it. What you're really doing is subtly dropping it in your hand while the eye sees it being grabbed. Y'all, I am trying to tell you, I practiced this thing more than Michael Jordan did batting practice and Anna Mae sang "Nutbush City Limits." Like them, I came up empty. I performed the trick over and over but ten out of ten times, people always picked the hand I was supposed to "fool" them with. I was the worst.

I had to come to grips with the reality that being a magician was not in the cards for me (see what I did there?). I realized I needed to change my expectations. Being a professional magician wasn't the path God had for me, but I could enjoy it as a hobby.

BLACKNESS REDEFINED

Throughout history, the Black experience has meant engaging in the practice of killing our emotions. This goes against God's design for us as people.

Emotion is defined as an instinctive or intuitive feeling distinguished from the reasoning of knowledge. I'm focusing on the "instinctive or intuitive feeling" aspect of the definition. For too long, we as a people did not have the freedom to express the deep well of our intuitions holistically. Society wedged us into a corner to erroneously set a course for us that was not of God's intended purpose. However, there are some icons who lived contrary to the norm of society; these were prophets such as Ida B. Wells, W. E. B. Du Bois, Carter G. Woodson, Malcolm X, Rev. Dr. Martin Luther King Jr., Medgar Evers, James Baldwin, Angela Davis, Lauryn Hill, Tom Skinner, Maya Angelou, Frederick Douglass, Nikki Giovanni, Toni Morrison, and many more. These heroes as well as many unnamed others are symbols of courage who gave voice to the emotions we have often felt.

Like me doing the coin drop, many of us have tried over and over and over to master a way of life that is not for us. The reality is this: God made us a mighty people group who are creatively prophetic in nature, but our attempts to stifle that emotion in response to injustice and defeat have been the collective death of us. Yes, we have the Nina Simone types whose art and protest are indistinguishable, but music is not where life is lived for most of us. It is, however, a cry of the soul—the souls of people like her who were not surrounded by a community that supported them.

Blackness redefined means we refuse to be different from our authentic selves or to convey an emotion different from what we intuitively know to be true and are designed to express. Because of the traditions killing our freedom both outwardly and inwardly, we have a skewed view of humanity and Blackness, and it must change. We must see the actual condition of ourselves. People like

Spike Lee leaked these intuitions into films in an attempt to improve our state of Black identity. We need to know our true condition; it is the reason we must change.

CHEAT CODE NO. 5

We must change the way we relate to each other emotionally and sexually, we must change the way we handle those in pain, and we must be careful what identities we try to put on or take from others. Black men cannot leave their Black women behind and call it progression. Black men and women must refrain from cannibalizing each other due to the trauma comparison of who had it worse.

We are powerful creatures, and God gave us powerful emotions to express our needs. Like me with the coin drop, we can practice over and over and pretend like this is the path God has for us—or we can stop and get on the path of healing and change.

> **Black men and women must refrain from cannibalizing each other due to the trauma comparison of who had it worse.**

Don Furious told me I was in pain and that this pain had become a badge of honor in my community. In order to earn it, though, I had to ignore and endure; this was antithetical to God's hope for me. That day, more lights came on for me. I realized I needed to call out this problem and change the direction our people had walked in for centuries, calling it following God.

This is not God or Blackness. It is what Lauryn Hill says in her song "I Get Out": "traditions killin' freedom." The refusal to recognize our condition and the need for change has killed many of us for too long.

HISTORICAL REFLECTION

I remember the first time I read about Ida B. Wells in James Cone's *The Cross and the Lynching Tree*. I was captivated and compelled by her willingness to change the status quo and hold accountable both white and Black churches that did not speak out against the lynching of Black people. Her life struck a chord as she challenged people to understand that a life lived with Christ could not focus on the spiritual component of the person while ignoring the physical realities happening around them. Even when she received no support from a number of Black and white churches due to the fear and tyranny prevalent at the time, Wells persisted in changing the course and path for her people.

Her legacy continues today. She stood for calling people to put their gospel to the test in a volatile society even if it cost you your life. She did not allow people to believe they were Christians in spirit while ignoring what was happening in the physical society (especially when many of the lynchings were done by churchgoers and church leaders). She called people to live an integrated gospel of the kingdom.

CHEAT CODE NO. 6

The biggest revelation Don Furious gave me was the need for me to live as an integrated person. He wrote down the different components of a person: the spirit, the soul, the mind, the psyche, the physical actions, the eyes, and the deepest gut feelings we have. He said the person who lives as one, successfully and consistently bringing all these pieces of themselves together, experiences God's joy. This person lives as one person every day in every situation of their life. If this freedom is robbed from you and your people, you reproduce bondage and nothing more.

Don said, "Adam, you only know one part of freedom: living to provide as survival, and that part has been met with shame and uncertainty."

> **Blackness redefined rejects the "traditional" belief that we must conceal and edit pieces of ourselves.**

I believe we need to start asking the question, what does it mean to live integrated, and how is it achieved? How are your thoughts and feelings realized without the shame of wondering, "What if someone knew I did this or thought this way?" To live in this fear is to disintegrate yourself.

Don went on to say, "I believe no one can thrive with this type of existence. God has not called us to live fractured and disintegrated lives but integrated and abundant lives."

Blackness redefined rejects the "traditional" belief that we must conceal and edit pieces of ourselves for acceptance and progression. We see the landscape of our personhood and know we must change. We believe we will live integrated lives, and any relationship that does not allow us to bring the full person through the door is not worth having. We must refuse to cower and hope for acceptance but trust God with the full expression of ourselves. Black folks have a prophetic essence from God designed to bless all of humanity when unhindered. We must reject the traditional voice that says, "Life cannot be lived unless I fracture and disintegrate myself." You are a whole person, and here is your permission to be so.

Make Change (A Spoken Word)

Broken glass *everywhere*
Piece by piece I mend what I *can*
Insufficient these hands of mine
Work using the only tools they know
For *restoration.*
Provision is the *means*
Yet my emotions *scream*
I am a part of this *process*
Sit your five-dollar ass down before
I make *change*
I must *change*

Knowing our condition
Is the reason we must change
Bringing what was normal and scattered
Back to the intent of the designer, as one, *oneness.*
Traditions kill freedom
God kills myths for us to be *free*
Transformation is not based on information alone
Information does not transform the emotions.
WE CAN CHANGE.

CHAPTER 5

THE PRICE IS WRONG

It's freedom time!

One cold LA morning at 4 a.m. my wife asks, "Can you get me something to eat?" She's pregnant with Zipporah, our first child, so I grit my teeth and get to it.

I take off walking like Denzel in *The Book of Eli*. This is before Yelp is a thing, so the whole time I'm thinking, *Where in the hell will I get food at 4 a.m.? Nothing is open—well, nothing that won't kill me.* All I can do is ask God to show me where to walk since nothing is lit up.

Then, like a true revelation from God, I see a bright light in the hazy darkness. There are people walking toward the light, so I proceed that way too until I see a building. It doesn't look like a place where there's food, but I think the steady traffic of people could lead to food.

As I get closer, I see signs everywhere that say "I.L.Y.M." As I try to decipher what I.L.Y.M. is, I see more signs that read, "Casting this way." Eventually I see people carrying wardrobe items. I am in the flow of people and suddenly a guy yells out, "Extras this way!" I thank him and follow the crowd. From a distance, I see the answer to my prayers: a table covered with *food*.

The reason my wife and I are out at 4 a.m. in the first place is that we've been waiting in line to get into today's taping of *The Price Is Right*. But by now I've figured out that I.L.Y.M. stands for *I Love You, Man*, a big-time Hollywood movie. I'm thinking, *I love Bob Barker and Drew Carey like the rest, but we have been out here too long, my wife is pregnant, she's hungry, and our chances of getting into the building—let alone on the show—are slim. And here's an opportunity to be extras in a legit movie starring Paul Rudd and Rashida Jones—plus food! What else could we ask for?*

This seems like God's abundant answer to prayer, but just in case I ask if a "food establishment" is open. Everyone gives me a look, then someone points out the food right in front of us. I explain that my wife is picky, and they point me to a diner across the street. As I leave, I formulate a plan in my head. I will get these greasy-spoon pancakes with onion residue in them and bring them to my wife, even though she won't eat them, and I'll tell her about the incredible guaranteed opportunity of food and movie fame we can have if we reconsider our plans for the day. I am sure God wants us to leave the line we're in—but it's one of those days where you feel disappointment is inevitable.

I bring my wife the pancakes with the onion residue. Like any other woman who is pregnant, she takes two bites of this food she "needed" and is repulsed by it. But I digress. I try to convince her to get on board with my grand plan for stardom, but she shuts it down.

"No, babe, we going to get on *Price Is Right*," she says.

"*The Price Is Right* is not promised, though," I plead. "This is, and there is *real food*, and it is a *legit movie!*"

She stands firm, and that feeling of inevitable disappointment returns.

So we wait. Six a.m. comes and goes, 7 a.m. comes and goes, then 9 a.m. and 10 a.m. People are being let in, and we can finally see the front of the line where people are entering. Unbeknownst to my wife and me, we are in line for the taping of a huge celebration show. There is a rule that if parties of thirty or more show up later than individuals already in line, they automatically get on the show. This helps fill the crowd and provides storytelling opportunities. (Insert eye roll emoji.) So you know what happens next.

As we get closer to the entrance, a party of forty pulls up in a charter bus and is escorted to the front of the line. Our hearts sink. The staff tries to encourage us, saying we will probably still get in, but we know the sting of "no" is inevitable. Yet we hold out hope. By this time the sun is up and has chased away the cold. It's warm, but hunger is returning. Of course I remember the free food and the movie extra opportunity we turned down. We continue to wait.

There are thirty people in front of us, and that number slowly dwindles down to twenty, then fifteen, then eleven, then nine, then seven, and then five. We get our hopes up and think with excitement that we might make it in! We're down to two people in front of us, and the staff says they're putting out chairs because they really want to get us in. Finally, the two people in front of us are let in, and we are at the front of the line.

"Come on, man," I plead. "Let this rope down and let us into the show to bid *one dollar*." The man leaves for a moment, then returns with the same look Kanye had before he declared that George Bush didn't like Black people.

"I am sorry, but that is all we can take," he says.

I try the "my wife is pregnant" defense, to no avail. After all that waiting the inevitable happens: nothing.

I have never felt so empty. We felt like Theo when he watched Cockroach get selected for *Dance Mania* without him: drained and completely dejected. We tried to get over to the free movie food. Gone. What about still being an extra in the movie? Filming already in progress. *It was the biggest miss of my creative life.* All because I listened to the voice of my wife. (Love you, babe!)

> **We felt like Theo when he watched Cockroach get selected for *Dance Mania* without him: drained and completely dejected.**

Waiting in line for *The Price Is Right* is not a fun experience. You get up entirely too early with the hopes of getting something that is not promised, and your order in line predicts the attention you get. To make it worse, people can jump in front of you because there are made-up rules that determine that these people are more important than you.

BLACKNESS REDEFINED

I remember sitting with Don Furious when he asked me a five-word question: "What is your birth order?" He said birth order matters, and—sad to say—if you are not in the front of the birth line, you tend to not get the best.

I told him I am the youngest of three, and I gave him the context of living in Detroit and having my dad leave us when I was twelve. This was despite the fact that, two years earlier, I'd asked him if he and my mom were going to divorce, and he told me no. Six months after my father left, my mother was severely wounded by a gunshot. Two years later, my sister got pregnant with my nephew. Sometime after that, I discovered I was the unplanned child.

After hearing all of that, Don Furious said, "God wants you alive because you should be dead." He went on to say, "You should be dead in every way: physically, spiritually, mentally, and emotionally."

Later Don's wife, Renee (also a counselor), told me I have "orphan syndrome." I was the child who was left over and over because of all the craziness that happened once my father exited. When my nephew came along, he was treated more like a sibling, so I wasn't cared for like I needed. "Nothing against your mother," she said, "but your birth order and the traumas that created these wounds matter."

In redefining my Blackness I had to understand that birth order mattered. Being part of a people who have known fighting and struggling to survive their place in line meant that the amount of energy your parents brought to the task of raising you could vary. You often heard the legitimate phrase "I'm tired" and you knew it wasn't from work but from the life lived through emotional and spiritual stress. So being the youngest of three with said tired mother defines a way of life.

HISTORICAL NOTE

We have not sat enough with the "birth order" of our legacy of being descendants of enslaved Africans. Being brought here against their will landed our ancestors in a societal ethnic birth order that inflicted hundreds of traumas upon them, and the effects of those traumas continue to be passed down from generation to generation.

Imagine a woman in northern Ghana who is three months into her pregnancy. Suddenly she hears her village being raided. She and her family hide in raid caves, but she and her husband are still captured. They're now in distress, along with other men, women, and children. They are sold for cowrie shells then whipped and forced to march over five hundred miles south to the slave castles on the western coast. They march, and this pregnant woman feels all of this in her body. A few miles from the coast, she and the others are told to bathe naked in a nearby river. It will be their last bath before arriving at one of the slave castles: Elmina or Cape Coast.

At the slave castle, hundreds of kidnapped Africans are processed and placed in dungeons where they live most of their lives in total darkness, lying in funk and waste. Above the dungeons is a chapel where Dutch Christians worship and drown out the sounds of their cries for help. This woman, now six months pregnant, is chained at the bottom of a slave ship and endures the Middle Passage, a voyage to the Americas. It is a voyage of rocky seas and horrid conditions. They arrive on the shores of Jamestown, where she, her husband and children, and others are stripped naked and placed on an auction block. She is now seven months pregnant. One by one, she watches as her family members are sold and separated, probably never to see each other again. She does not have the words to describe what she's feeling: depression, trauma, catastrophe, distress. But her body and her unborn baby are feeling every bit of it. She eventually gives birth to her child on a plantation.

When I tell this story (the first time was on a panel hosted by Yale for mental health), I ask people if they think the child in the womb was affected by the stressful situations mom went through. One hundred percent of the time, they silently agree the baby felt it all. When we talk about prenatal care, we usually focus on food, physical well-being, and so on. Rarely do we address emotional prenatal care. Why do I share this? Because we ignore with

> **Corporately, our birth order is that of the child who never received love like the other children.**

anemic ignorance the four hundred years of stress and emotional trauma Black people and especially pregnant Black women experienced and have never considered how it has affected children in the womb. Corporately, our birth order is that of the child who never received love like the other children. This is experienced in the womb as well as in our firsthand experiences.

CHEAT CODE NO. 7

Birth order matters, from a familial standpoint and societal one. The conversation I had with Don Furious was a cheat code for me. I literally felt the pain in my chest and gut dissolve as someone gave language to what I had felt most of my life. Don Furious told me on many occasions that I don't believe anyone loves me because my needs beyond the provisional level didn't get met in my family or in the community where I grew up. This wound became my norm as I faced a continual onslaught of trauma.

I eventually came to the "revelation" that life was easier when navigated solo. I needed nurturing that life didn't give me. Because of my order in the family line, I never felt important. In fact, it was communicated in some ways that I wasn't important. This wasn't based on a motive but on a grid determined through trauma of who got the best—and that was not me. Don told me my trauma programmed me to make it hard to hear the truth that I am loved and worthy of someone's best. I could not hear this truth because my programming had taught me the opposite.

You think your programming is the truth, but it is not. That is trauma distorting realities into a lie—the abnormal into the normal. This is not God's best for me, for you, or for any of our people. Therefore, we must do the work of healing. Satan (and many times we ourselves) will double down on attempts to make these unprocessed realities life. He will try to convince you these experiences are God's best for you. They are not.

The cheat code I learned that day with Don Furious and later with his wife, Renee, is that birth order not only matters; it's vital. This helped me understand why the lingering voices of accusations ("You are not worth anyone's best," "Be like your other siblings," "You must figure life out alone," "God won't give you his best," "Just endure until heaven comes") were the loudest voices in my head.

I believe my Blackness—and Blackness in America—is defined by who can endure the most pain without processing and admitting that it hurts, even to the death of our bodies. Blackness also misses that our birth order in this country has been the least and we've accepted that. What would it look like if we didn't puff our chests out at who could internalize and "endure" the most pain without processing it? What if we grieved our familial and historical birth orders while charting a new course and path? What if healing and integrated wholeness as a people were the aim instead of unprocessed trauma causing a lifelong internal war that affects the body?

> **Blackness in America is defined by who can endure the most pain without processing and admitting that it hurts.**

I call it "Black Panther suit living." We absorb the shots from life and the opposition over and over and over; eventually, those realities we absorb come out and do damage. However, this is not a script. Sadly, the damage—mistargeted energy—is done against our loved ones and our bodies.

Most of my life I felt my chest wanting to explode. It seemed reasonable because we called it the Blues, rap, great art, and culture. In reality, it was unprocessed trauma impacting me mentally, spiritually, and psychologically. Through kingdom therapy, I came to discover it wasn't

Blackness. It was an unhealthy life. Instead of making me strong, the Black card was really killing me. I experienced decades of internalized trauma—from the violence of protecting myself to racism and discrimination to being neglected when I needed nurturing.

During this time my body was screaming, "*Help!* Release this madness! *Talk, fool!*" But I did not have the words. My people never had the words or space; at one time, we literally never had the freedom.

I write this to give hope to the reader that he or she will find language for the experiences of carrying unprocessed trauma. I want you to experience the same freedom I did, the freedom to be able to express your feelings of pain and hurt. When you have language, there is a tangible way toward joy and healing. A promise I stand on and offer to you is this: "Out of your darkness, your void, Eden can and will come."

Lauryn Hill in her song "Freedom Time" talks about "Truth come, we can't hear it when you've been programmed to fear it." This truth I was programmed to hear was mostly a lie, but I was programmed to fear the truth I needed to hear. This was the light I needed to break through in the darkest time in my life. As I write this, I sit in the most joyful time of my life but am still on the road to healing. You have the permission to walk the path of healing and expand your understanding of strength and Blackness.

Arise (A Spoken Word)

Arise from the pious prayers and posture of
    God *please*
Refuse to purchase products that
Cushion your *knees*
You have the answers to the test
And is it not *you*
It is a community beyond the scope
And the knowledge that you are accustomed *to*
It comes through the voices that you have been told
    to *discard*
Real trauma repackaged and sold at
A premium that you and your community have
    purchased and called it
IDENTITY
As you stand and fight for the badges and medals
    that honor you among your *brethren*
your soul withers
You continue the piety of waiting for a God
    Superman that is not *coming*
But something greater has *come*
Your deceptive programming gave you a code of
    beliefs that health is anti-everything you
    stand *for*
Yes, it is *anti*
Anti-*ego*

Anti-*pain*
Anti-*cowardice*
Anti-*internalization*
And all things slavery and *fear*
Accept the form of freedom outside of the stifling
    standards stashed steep within your *cells*

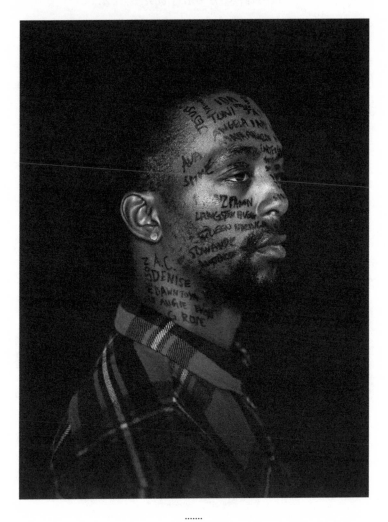

CHAPTER 6

THE MASTERMIND

Master's in mass confusion.

*/E·mo·tion·al trans·par·en·cy/ n. Being able to
associate pain with what you are feeling.*

I was ten years old, but I can still remember it like it
was yesterday. I can still see the terrible all-blue
room my brother and I shared—light-blue walls
and navy-blueish baseboards. The comforter I slept under
in the cold Detroit winters and the box fan we put in the
window during the hot Detroit summers? You guessed it,
both blue.

I also remember when I found out Satan was real. I lay
under my covers, and for the first time I felt a suffocating
presence hover over my chest, pushing me into the mat-
tress. I peeked my head out to see if it was my brother, but
I could hear him sleeping. I then pulled my head back

under my comforter and pulled the blanket tightly around me. I was gripped with fear, wondering what this feeling wanted. So I did what I was taught to do: Say the name of Jesus . . . at least that's what I tried to do.

The movie *Beetlejuice* comes to mind here. Michael Keaton fans remember the scene toward the movie's climax when everyone is trying to send Beetlejuice away. All they had to do to send him away was say his name three times, right? But in that scene, Beetlejuice did everything in his power to keep them from uttering his name three times.

There I was, under my covers, and I thought to myself, *I will verbalize what I have been taught. Say Jesus' name, and the devil flees.* However, just like in *Beetlejuice*, it was like the presence—Satan, his henchmen, whoever—knew if I spoke Jesus' name aloud, the authority of his name would force them to leave. I tried the hardest I could and felt like a kid fighting Deebo from *Friday*. It was like someone had stapled my lips shut and shot my jaws with a paralysis drug that kept them from opening. While my mind was saying the name, I was scared and pale under the covers. Still I could not get my lips and jaws open to say the name. It was a helpless position to be in. I prayed with fervor in my mind because I knew God was all-knowing. I prayed and I prayed until I passed out and woke up the next morning. I remember thinking, *I don't know how Satan interacts with us, but this force is real and hates to hear the name of Jesus uttered.* This was not the last time something like this happened.

Fast-forward two decades later. I am on a flight to Washington and ferociously devouring an audiobook recommended by Don Furious, *The Body Keeps the Score.* It all hits me at one time. The book contextualized research from other books I'd read like *Soul of Shame* and *Anatomy of the Soul,* as well as Dr. Caroline Leaf's kingdom insights on detoxing your brain, neuroplasticity, and how Satan manipulates our thinking. It all came to a head. I thought, *No way, he really is a deceiver. . . . F**k Satan. He hates us. . . . His plans started even when we didn't have the tools to respond.*

Many people have differing views on Satan—what he looks like, how he fell, whether he fell, and everything in between. I will say this: we have a literal adversary, and his plans to destroy do not start when you are ready for the battle. This is what makes him the coward he is. Be it me as a clueless child or someone prepped and ready with "the full armor" of Ephesians 6:11, the enemy wants to destroy and will wait you out or come unexpected when you are young.

We have a literal adversary, and his plans to destroy do not start when you are ready for the battle.

What is the reality and code here?

CHEAT CODE NO. 8A

There are many codes, but the core revelation is this: Satan is not merely a force trying to affect our spiritual disposition; he wants to ruin us at the deepest level. He's coming for our soul—and even wants to ruin us at the cellular level of who we are from inception. This evil being does not care when it starts. There is no "age of innocence" to him. It is often, always, and at any time.

All these authors I read, in their own words, were saying something similar: Satan uses your past traumas and wounds to convince you your future will be no better. His deception is best at giving you a false predictability for your life. In some ways he strengthens and conditions you to be a false prophet of your own life. Therefore, if abandonment is all you've known, then your mind will predict a future of abandonment. If all you've known is neglect and the absence of nurturing, then your mind will predict a future of neglect where nurturing is not an option.

According to Dr. van der Kolk, author of *The Body Keeps the Score*, it is possible to train your brain to believe that different outcomes can happen, and it comes from giving your mind and body new associations. I am no expert, but it was freeing to see Dr. Caroline Leaf explain and show at the cellular level how toxic ruminating on the past actually destroys cells in your physical brain and spreads to your body. It was even more amazing to learn how God reverses and renews your body and mind on the cellular level. It put the entire Bible into a visible light that I was previously incapable of seeing. I was like *Dang! God is amazing!* I also recognized that Satan is a cruel torture specialist who knows how the mind works and what it defaults to. He reminds us of our past as often as he can and uses it against us, leading us to believe something that is not true based on the engineering of our bodies or on God's love.

Satan really does have what Lauryn Hill would call "PhDs in illusion, master's of mass confusion, bachelor's in past illusion." He operates on past memories only to have us predict a false future absent of hope.

BLACKNESS REDEFINED

I saw the war and illusions for what they were and God for who he is and how he works. He can function as a silver bullet, but he has also engineered the body with tools to heal holistically. These are tools our real enemy does not want us to know about. What I am about to say may sound harsh, but it's a conversation I believe is overdue for those of us in the Black community. Too often, the Black church and Blackness have sought to sing and pray away problems that were holistic in nature. So when the problems didn't go away, one needed deliverance. But we never understood the full composition of our humanity. We weren't addressing the pains and needs of our whole person.

Satan does understand, and he doesn't care what we know as he cloaks his intentions to destroy us. Rabbi David Fohrman shares a great breakdown of the Hebrew word *erom*, which can mean both "nakedness" and "cunning" given the context. In his book *The Beast That Crouches at the Door*, he says:

> When someone is naked *[erom]*, unclothed, there is no hiding. That person's self is laid bare for all to see. . . . On the other hand, when one is cunning *[erom]*, he is sly and devious; he "cloaks" his true intentions and hides behind a façade.

So before the fall, while Adam and Eve were both *erom* (naked) and unashamed, the beast of the field was *erom* (cloaked, cunning, crafty, and sly). I use this to drive home the point of Satan being *erom*, cloaked. His plans are cloaked. His intentions to destroy are cloaked. All of his ways are cloaked, hidden behind a façade of good with the end being our death and destruction.

CHEAT CODE NO. 8B

Satan's power is not in crafting something new; only God can create something out of nothing. All Satan can do is whisper in your ear and tell you that the traumas you have seen will remain as the standard of your life going forward. Once you settle into his lie and it disseminates into your brain as the truth—about your life and God—he has subtly robbed you of the greatest gift God gave us: hope. This isn't blind hope but hope in God. Satan has been running this scheme of misdirection since the Garden of Eden, and he continues the cycle today.

But we use words like "keeping it real" to remain mired in our pessimism. Jay-Z has a line in "Where I'm From" in which he talks about being from a place "where niggas been praying so long that they atheist." My theologian friends will rush to correct the line instead of understanding what he's emotionally communicating on behalf of many who live these lives. Black folks who grow up in war zones pray for it all to stop: the violence, the death, the hunger pains, the destruction. And while Yeshua (Jesus) may save us from hell, we still wake up in an earthly hellhole void of God's people who have resources to help us get out or change the situation. Jay is not an atheist, but like us all he was crying out for tangible wholeness beyond the pulpit and the four walls of a building. He was rapping about a need for real hope.

This hope kept Nat Turner from believing slavery was God's best for him. This hope kept Frederick Douglass believing slavery wasn't the end for him. The same hope kept Harriet Tubman leading the Underground Railroad. It kept Ida B. Wells writing and speaking out against lynching despite receiving minimal support from Black and white churches. It emboldened Robert Smalls to shed the chains of his slavery and sail himself and his loved ones through enemy waters to fight for freedom.

Black folks, we come from a line of people who have hoped against the odds. We also come from those who were too traumatized to hope because it was beaten out of them. And when it wasn't beaten out of them it was stolen and legislated away from them. But there is a new day—an awakening.

The standard has to be hope. Once hope is removed, we are at the whim of the enemy and our environment. Trauma is real and manifests itself in many ways, but the days of suppressing our stories need to be over. This suppression is an illusion of the highest mastery. It is not Blackness; it is death served sweet digested with bitter hooks hidden inside the morsels. Trauma is real, but so is restoration and hope to create new pathways in your brain that you have not experienced before. You have the permission to hope, to be Black and truly hope.

> **Black folks, we come from a line of people who have hoped against the odds.**

Have the Audacity (A Spoken Word)

The audacity to *hope*
My eyes are darkened by the past
Distress that appears to be the only
Images I can make out as what I am *worth*.

Worth comes from what I am reminded *of*
Stuck on replay like a record scratching and
    skipping back to the same part of the song
    that reminds me
I am no *good*
I am left to my own devices of eating fruit and
    being my personal *God*
Good things don't happen to people like *you*
And bad things don't happen to good *people*
Both accusations land square upon the bullseye of
    my conscience reminding me . . .
Just reminding *me* . . .
The audacity to hope in something that I have never
    seen is *maddening*
Maddening
All I hear and see is *darkness*
No roads, no paths, just *darkness*
Out of darkness, not in, but out of the darkness
    came the best creation and *Eden*
Colors we have never *seen*
The beautiful came from the *unseen*
The beauty that we now *see*
The bodies we pine and salivate after
Came from a canvas and model of the *unknown*
A *void*
Nothing before . . . and hidden *mold*
The glorious foods that set our

Taste buds *arise*

Didn't come from a filed construction of

Leftover foods *known*

But the *unseen*

When darkness is all you see

Then Eden is the only option that God can give *you*

Hope in God, not in a new situation

Based off of the old *ceasing*

But in a unique situation that breaks and pinnacles
the *old*

With no connection to the *past*

The audacity to hope in *God*

Who set a reminder down to the very creation of
oxygen in our *bodies*

The air we breathe was once not in *existence*

The verve we have comes not from a blueprint

But the darkest night that is a canvas

for the marvelous *new*

HAVE THE AUDACITY . . .

CHAPTER 7

WHERE IS MY CAR?

Name the pain.

I remember when I got my first car. It wasn't a Benz or a Lambo, but for all of my emotion, you would have thought it was. My mother decided to ease my burden of having to rely on the city bus for transportation. Those long nights in the Detroit streets because of sports can have a mother's mind spinning, so she decided to get me what I thought was and still is the holy grail of hood cars: *a box Regal.*

My uncle and mother dropped $2,000 on a 1988 navy-blue Buick Regal. When I came home and saw that car in the driveway, it was like the whole world stopped. I saw imaginary sparkles gleaming from the car in slow motion. I walked into the house with one question looming in my head, and out it came: "Mom, whose car is that?"

I wondered if someone was visiting, or . . . dare I even hope? My mother responded with words that I will never forget: "It. Is. Yours."

All the things I could do with this car! I could get all the girls I wanted because of the identity it falsely infused in my ego. I could put up forty in a game because I had a Regal. I would look like a G because I had a Regal. (Oh, the mind of a teen boy with his first car.) I conjured up all these things that a car can't actually deliver, and guess what? None of those things happened. Of course!

I did have my times of "flossing" through the city streets, and life was glorious for a good minute. Cats asked for rides, and I happily said yes so I could drive around and let other cats see my head in the driver's seat as I cruised past these less-than-stylish folks. *I. Had. The. Regal.* Right now, if one of my ideas brought me billions, you know what type of car I would buy. So yes, I had my "all about me" time. I was even sure to use the Club so my car wouldn't be stolen. I settled into having the car. I overwashed it and instead of the obligatory practice of renting a vehicle you couldn't afford, I drove it to homecoming. And then it happened.

I was living at my dad's house during this stint of my life during high school. One morning I opened the front door as I prepared for my a.m. ride to practice and another day of flossing. I walked out to the usual spot where my car was parked and I cannot explain to you how the empty space where my car was supposed to be matched the emptiness in my gut. I rushed back into the house, clinging to a sliver of hope as I asked a question I already knew the answer to: "Dad, did you move my car by chance?"

No. I told him to go outside and tell me what he saw. He took a walk, looked out front and out back, came back, and told me he saw nothing. Then he yelled to my stepmother, "Mel, Adam's car has been stolen."

I will never forget that moment when he verbalized my reality. My car had been stolen. My stepmother, a cop at the time, gave me some semblance of hope that it would be recovered. But that car in the Detroit area was more valuable than vibranium. By this time it was already stripped and processed. Life was over for me. My identity and world were gone. What would I do now? I was like Alonzo in *Training Day:* "You think you can do this to me?"

To this day the thing that stung wasn't the car being stolen, it was hearing my dad verbalize the reality that I did not want to face: "Adam's car has been stolen."

BLACKNESS REDEFINED

In her song "I Get Out," Lauryn Hill says there is a way about life and trauma that has us living in a state of psychosis where we have "psychological locks . . . repressing true expression, cementing this repression . . . so that no one can be healed."

One of the exercises Don Furious gave to help me mourn and grieve the traumas and wounds I internalized was "naming the pain." (This is not what he called it but what I call it.) He would ask me a series of questions, and I was supposed to respond not with information but with the name of an emotion. He started with my dad. What emotion or word did I feel when I thought of him? He then went down a list, naming my mom, brother, sister, the city of Detroit, my middle school and high school, shootings, divorce, college, church, white church, and so on. He went down the list of *everything*.

I shared with him freely, and he showed me the words I chose. Next he asked me if I'd felt the freedom to express this and if I'd processed any of this hurt. I had not; it had never been an option. He said, "Do you see?"

I did! I let it out, not then but in my time of homework and studies. I removed the emotional dam and the flood of healing tears came. This was the best thing I had ever done, and still, I have to practice not internalizing situations. I redefined another element of Blackness that day: to name and grieve the pain.

CHEAT CODE NO. 9

I learned that if I didn't grieve the past, none of my relationships in the present would ever have a clean and fair slate. I wouldn't be able to make space to love someone and be in an imperfect relationship with them. They would unknowingly have to fight against many unresolved wounds and tirelessly try to work themselves out of a hole. They would also try to fill a void they couldn't ever possibly fill. Only the Lord can fill these holes through his healing process.

> **I learned that if I didn't grieve the past, none of my relationships in the present would ever have a clean and fair slate.**

If you don't name the pain, you will think you are living in the present while chained to your wounded past. Ignoring something and simply moving forward without healing is not health and is far from the truth.

Don Furious also explained to me why I all of a sudden became extremely sleepy—bedtime at 8 p.m. sleepy. When I started naming, grieving, and healing from pain, he said, "The Lord made the body to naturally flow like a river, and what trauma does in creating wounds is it convinces you to start building dams to hold back your emotions. That's internalization. When you start to name the pain, you remove the dam, and your emotions flow freely as they were intended. The body then starts to rejuvenate and recover back to its predetermined state." My body was healing and getting free from all the emotions I had buried, and sleep was its way of repair.

This brother kept giving me the infinity stones to health and kingdom healing every time I talked to him, and I am passing it on to you. If there were a sale on clothes and shoes, I would tell you. Well, God is allowing one person to discover tools that have been withheld and unrecognizable to our community for centuries. There is a *free sale on healing, y'all!*

Dr. Caroline Leaf talks about internalization of trauma reaching down to the cellular level of the brain and body. She talks about how cells start to die off when we don't name the pain, internalize it, and then live as if that pain is what the entire world thinks and believes of us.

Christ asked the demons in the Gerasene demoniac, "What is your name?" The response was, "My name is Legion, for we are many." Christ did not let them linger in this man. He ordered them by name out of this man. Then they went into the pigs and the pigs drowned (Mark 5:1-17).

CHEAT CODE NO. 10

I will say that my people, Black folks, live in a state Lauryn Hill describes as "psychological locks . . . repressing true expression, cementing this repression . . . so that no one can be healed." I believe God wants us to be free.

Don Furious told me, "The work to ignore and not name the pain is actually harder to do than dealing with the pain and becoming whole. You are comfortable with the routine of pain. You are convinced, through the code of Blackness, that blocking out the pain is freedom and a sign of strength. You will never be free until your entire story can be a communication of hope."

Sheesh! (Insert exploding brain emoji.)

The best work names the pain, removes the dams, and lets the rivers of our inner selves flow for true healing. Any other process is a dam—a method of internalizing. Not naming the pain is actually a hindrance to seeing Christ work in your life.

This is about the emotions of what you have felt but have lacked the words to describe in many cases. Life's circumstances didn't afford you the opportunity to process the feelings. Emotions are worth a thousand words. In the reality of Black folks, these words legally and societally traumatized us, keeping us from true expression.

> **Not naming the pain is actually a hindrance to seeing Christ work in your life.**

You have the permission to remove your dams and repair from the cellular level.

Name (A Spoken Word)

A *name*
There is so much in a *name*
A simple *name*
It is the declaration of what you believe a child will *be*
It is the statement of what you want your business
        and product to stand
For
So much in a *name*
Imagine a child growing up
And not knowing what to call his or herself but boy
        and *girl*

Not Zion, David, Deborah, or *Jael*
There is power to a *name*
Even pain deserves a *name*
Not to linger and be a reminder
But to be dealt with and *dissolved*
Neglect, you did hurt, and I mourn you
And now I close that *door*
Prejudice from the religious, you did *hurt*
I cry that reality and
You are *dissolved*
There is so much in a *name*
What are the names of pains that
Mingle in your head and body that
Refuse to go because you have not
Named the obvious but pretend it is
Not *there*
Name the *pain*
Mourn to *heal*
Dissolve those dams that dare to damn us to silence
        and *despair*
Emancipate the fullness of God's intended *design*

CHAPTER 8

NEW RULES, NEW LOVE

Arguing with compassion.

*/Con·scious/ adj. Aware of and responding
to one's surroundings; awake.*

hat we see is not in tandem with what we feel. Wounds are not made in a vacuum.

I argued ferociously with my wife about something I cannot even remember as I type this. Isn't that how it always goes? But in that moment, I am mad. The true feeling, though, is hurt, but I dare not admit it. I do remember the pain of feeling left out. It isn't her fault, but my childish and cowardly ways want her to feel pain. I don't want to risk letting her in and ending up hurt like so many situations in the past. So there I am, hurling accusation after accusation.

"This is just like growing up in Detroit!" "You talk like my mother used to!"

I have no idea how the argument resolved itself, but at this time of unhealthy living, it was easy to convince myself I was right because of my internalized and unprocessed trauma—Black Panther suit living. I believed no one, including my wife, could be for me. I used childish ways, like the silent treatment, to shut her out. I didn't realize my pain had nothing to do with her. It was about a truth I didn't want to accept or admit—people could hurt me. To admit this was a sign of weakness.

I brought this issue of toxic arguing to Don Furious. I asked him if there was such a thing as a healthy disagreement, one where the two parties didn't create trauma and leave wounds. His response forever changed how I view tension and "back and forth" conversations.

CHEAT CODE NO. 11

Don Furious said, "Most people are not healthy. . . . Most people, when they argue, are behaving in a way influenced by decades of unprocessed traumas that have nothing to do with the current individual. But they don't realize it."

"How will I know when I am healthy and healed from these past traumas?" I asked.

"When you are arguing with compassion and not with imperatives and facts about the other. Compassion goes beyond the conscious level and believes the heart of the individual even when their imperfect actions say otherwise," he said. "But when the pains below the surface—the deeper pains—are not healed, you won't trust anyone's motives and intentions on a deeper level. . . . It is impossible because you have your traumas and wounds with an enemy telling you not to trust, and you will listen every time if you are not healed. Unhealed trauma that is triggered is too strong a force to resist."

I remember sitting in the chair feeling like this dude had just read all my mail and wondering if he was about to ascend into heaven like an angel. Lauryn Hill asks a question in her song "I Get Out": "Who made up these rules? I say . . . animal conditioning , oh, just to keep us as a slave. . . . Oh, just get out."

BLACKNESS REDEFINED

I left that talk with Don Furious thinking I needed to grieve like never before. I especially needed to grieve the things I could remember because I wanted my wife to have a clean slate. I wanted her to be free to be imperfect and not have to be confronted by my unhealed past. I do believe this is the current state of most folks I know as the result of our culture as Black folks. Old, unhealed wounds become an army the other person has to fight regularly when, in reality, the disagreement is really play fighting at best.

It is possible to heal. I remember getting to places where I could have a dialogue with my wife in the present because I one hundred percent believed she was for me. Our discussions became more about being in sync than being at war. I learned to stop seeing my wife as Jeffery Dahmer meets rival gang leader from Detroit who was plotting for my downfall. She ceased to be the random pit bull sniffing for the scent of fear coming off a kid walking down the street so she could run after him for blood. (Yeah, this happened in real life many times. Stray dogs, even Lassie, trigger my trauma.)

CHEAT CODE NO. 12

Arguing with compassion and not with facts means you refuse to allow situations to bring you to the cliff of your emotions. The new Blackness, healed, doesn't jump from that cliff anymore.

Throughout this book we've talked about the full historical legacy of why I, as a student and teacher of history, believe Black folks in America internalize so much. It is because we have been stuck in a reality that didn't afford us the space to process our personhood. We instead internalized our pain as a way to survive.

In his 1754 book *Some Considerations on the Keeping of Negroes*, John Woolman, a Quaker preacher and early abolitionist, writes about the societal, legacy-leaving impact slaveholders had on their children:

Humility and meekness are supernatural traits and so is love for your neighbor.

It appears, by experience, that where children are educated in fullness, ease and idleness, evil habits are more prevalent, than in common among such who are prudently employed in the way of so great temptation, but have also the opportunity of lording it over their fellow creatures, and being masters of men in their childhood, how can we hope otherwise than that their tender minds will be possessed with thoughts too high for them? Which, by continuance, gaining strength, will prove, like a slow current, gradually separating them from (of keeping from acquaintance with) that humility and meekness in which alone lasting happiness can be enjoyed.

Woolman is asking how the Christians of the time can expect their children to learn the ways of owning other humans while having ease and idleness but also being mindful of spiritual things higher than them, such as humility and meekness. Humility and meekness are supernatural traits and so is love for your neighbor—which would be the slave. According to Woolman in 1754, this reality of owning others did not just affect older minds but would shape the legacy of children, who would eventually become adults and perpetuate a deficient theological and sociological practice in lieu of a holistic study of the *imago Dei*.

Moreover, if you also think about this from the perspective of the enslaved and their future offspring, you can begin to understand how being owned would affect one's sense of agency. How difficult it must have been for our enslaved ancestors to develop the belief of being worth more than what a cruel and hypocritical society told them.

I believe that with the digitization of information shrinking the world, tools once unavailable to people of color to process their traumas are now available. Laws have changed, but make no mistake, traumas for Black folks are not entirely eradicated. They are not at the level and severity they once were, but the journey is far from over. If rehabilitation is a real thing, then processing wounds toward hope is essential. Otherwise, we're just managing external behaviors, and this will never set anyone free.

Our Blackness was rooted in rules of old that kept our people in bondage and kept us silent as we were just trying to stay alive. But we accepted what we were told about ourselves. It was a type of animal conditioning that now needs to be broken. There is so much more we need to break to set others free.

Frantz Fanon in his book *Black Skin, White Masks* says we need to stop looking to the white majority to find our identity. I would add we must look to God, who created us, to understand that our true trajectory is based on how he designed us and not on looking at what history took from a people group.

> **We must look to God, who created us, to understand our true trajectory.**

I reject the lies and remove myself from all the boxes. I reject basing my success on what whites have and not on what God has purposed for myself and my people. I reject how I was told to treat and oversexualize the Black woman. I reject how I was told to silence her, told to treat her as having just two sides, sensuality and strength. There was a time we accepted what was given to us for survival, helping the majority culture profit while eroding our people, but no more. I've decided to fill in the holes of trauma and live with compassion for the woman in front of me. You have permission to reject the boxes and live life in the present. To argue with compassion as a sign of Blackness redefined.

WAITING (A SPOKEN WORD)

Comprehend, what is perceived is not indicative of
    what is not *appreciated*
How, *Sway?*
Because your past does not have
The *answers*
Restoration *does*
As the past personifies itself *loud*
Responds with tears and names
Of *grief*
But I promise you that vocalization,
Will convert into whispers transitioning into
A dissolving muted voice

with no audio that will cease to *exist*
You will eventually divorce that
Unfaithful wife . . .
Getting out of that codependent relationship
of *ruse*
Wedding the one
Who has been patiently waiting
For you to drink from her garden of intense,
intimate unending intoxication . . .
Well-being.

CHAPTER 9

A LITTLE MOLD
WON'T KILL YOU

Past the disguise.

*/Sub·con·scious/ adj. Of or concerning the part
of the mind of which one is not fully aware, but
which influences one's actions and feelings.*

I remember when Don Furious broke it down to me
why people argue from the deficit they place their
loved ones in (see chapter eight). As we went deeper,
I realized how poisonous it was for me to be in relationships with others while I lived with unhealed pain.

I was "today years old" when I had a revelation. Just
hours after conversing with Don Furious and listening to
books about below-the-surface subconscious trauma, I
came across a video called "What You Need to Know
About Cutting Off the Molded Part of the Bread." It

talked about how the mold you see on the surface is just a small representation of what's ferociously growing under the surface. It showed a diagram of the spores and how long they had been spreading. It then explained that, while you only see the blue mold on one part of the surface, the reality is that the bread is consumed with mold.

I yelled, "So, cutting off the molded part of the bread does not keep mold from going into your body?" Cutting off the part of the bread that is blue doesn't do anything but give you peace of mind. In reality the entire slice is full of mold. This had been my lived experience for the entire thirty-seven years and 333 days of my life.

Besides being convinced to never eat molded bread again (which is a huge statement because I'll eat anything if it is not crawling), I realized this was what Don Furious meant when he talked about the good and bad below the surface. He said all of our actions have good and bad implications. These implications are more than what the person can see. The action may be one glaring spot while below the surface there is much more. You can observe a glaring action but fail to realize below the surface is unprocessed trauma. On the other end, you can mistake another person's imperfect action toward you to mean something more below the surface than what it is because *you* are not healed. An unhealthy person can read unhealthy motives even when they are not there. OK, mold analogy is over.

BLACKNESS REDEFINED

I came to the end of myself and had to give up this image of Blackness and false strength. I had to cry because not crying over pain was a badge I thought made me strong. In actuality, it was killing me and killing those around me. I felt by blocking things from my mind and not talking about them, cutting off the piece of the molded bread, was somehow keeping the rest of me healthy. I believed the rest of me was separate from the trauma and wounds spreading their way into the emotional cellular state of who I am.

> **An unhealthy person can read unhealthy motives even when they are not there.**

On the surface, people saw elements they would say were not good, but they didn't realize I was riddled with pain below the surface. Don Furious gave me a colossal cheat code to redefine my Blackness that day.

CHEAT CODE NO. 13

Don Furious gave me eyes to see that below the surface is the work many don't realize they have to do. This is true across all ethnicities, but historically speaking we as Black people have not been free to process our subconscious traumas. Yet the world expects us to perform as though those traumas never existed.

During the writing of this book, I've heard news about three Chicago police officers who were acquitted for the coverup in the killing of seventeen-year-old Laquan Mc-Donald as well as a white father and son who initially went uncharged in Georgia for shooting and killing twenty-five-year-old Ahmaud Arbery as he jogged through a neighborhood. These traumatic events demonstrate that our lives are still not valued. Not only are we not valued at an equal premium to whites; we're just not valued at all. If my people had the tools, the cheat codes, we could stop living as if Blackness meant just cutting off the piece of trauma and acting like it never existed. It hurts from Emmett Till to present day to see a judge not favor true justice for your people.

If we could find a new way of living, we could experience this conscious and subconscious integrated well-being. I believed then and still do today that this change will unleash the healthiest version of Black people upon the world.

This time with Don Furious showed me why my wife and I constantly missed each other on the conscious level. It taught me that our communication was negatively influenced by our unprocessed traumas and unhealed wounds. We were living as if the past didn't affect the present—or as if the subconscious didn't affect the conscious. I have news for you: they do. Our trauma and wounds are directly tied to the subconscious, which affects the conscious. No arguments or disagreements are had in an emotional vacuum if you have not healed.

I believe Blacks can heal in many ways for the first time in this country. We can do this with a new approach of seeing healthy families break cycles of trauma-based love, parenting, and legacy. Ignoring the pain below the surface doesn't have to be our story anymore.

> **Ignoring the pain below the surface doesn't have to be our story anymore.**

The most prominent subconscious voice I had to unearth was the one that said people only wanted to give me their "leftover" efforts in life. This voice had been on repeat since I was twelve. If people didn't respond to a text or invitation, I heard the voice reminding me people don't want to give me their best and I am not worth anyone's best. When Don Furious helped me unearth my trauma and wounds, I mourned them and healed. This allowed me to see my wife, children, and friends in a new light with peace and calm. I had a subconscious hole they were not responsible for, but I had unknowingly been putting pressure on them to fill it. It was my job to fill and repair the canyon. Sure, they could partner in it, but they could not fill it.

It was like I woke up from Satan's mind control. I stopped believing what he wanted me to believe and was finally able to see past the disguises and deception. I realized for the first time that everyone was not giving me their leftovers; I was loved. Love might come in an imperfect wrapping, but I was indeed loved despite what the surface looked like. *I was healed to believe and know* below the surface that *people were giving me their best, and they were for me.* You have permission to believe people are for you as part of a new form of Blackness.

NOURISHED (A SPOKEN WORD)

It grows *fast*
Being fed with the yeast of
Distressing *situation*
So subtle are the lenses of emotional
Distraught that casually and
Viciously kill us and those whom
We claim to *love*
We put ourselves at the center
Of others' deficiencies
Thinking their intentions
Are but *arsenic*
But in reality, we
Are the ones dressed in old lace
Needing new *attires*
Cutting off that piece won't make that
The bread you are holding on for nourishment
Give you *verve*

You need a fresh *loaf*
One that is more than taking away
The hunger pains within your *intestines*
New *sustenance*
One that grows life from *within*
Feeding thousands *externally*

CHAPTER 10

A NEW NARRATIVE

Being part of one's redemption story.

On that flight to Washington I mentioned earlier, all the lights of understanding came on as I listened to *The Body Keeps the Score*. I was flooded with decades of missed conversations with my siblings, friends, kids, and—the most important person—my wife. It was like God allowed hope to flash before my eyes. He allowed me into this world where I, like Amy Adams's character in *Arrival*, had the ability to access different points of time in my narrative to gain understanding.

This allowed me to understand how my current state impacted my levels of healing and hope. This understanding brought a close to two years of work—naming traumas, listening to a kingdom neurologist, listening to messianic rabbis, admitting people's ability to wound me, naming the moments when I lived in fear, naming the moments when I allowed pride to destroy me, and vow renewals—by giving a sharp sense of clarity. It gave me the tools to fight and win a war I didn't know was taking place. In that moment on the plane, it became clear. I would no longer be consciously and subconsciously victimized, because I now understood. Healing really can come. What am I talking about? Glad you asked . . .

In *The Body Keeps the Score*, Dr. Bessel van der Kolk describes the healing power of the top-down approach, which refers to the process of becoming aware of new information and tools to help your brain heal mentally and psychologically from emotional wounds you feel and images you see. However, when he talked about the bottom-up approach, I was undone. He explained how the body can take on new associations of positivity (and I would add hope), combat the old traumas, and replace them with new associations to heal itself.

In case you're sitting there like, "*Whaaat?*" let me explain. Let's take a "simple" traumatic trigger from my childhood: dogs. Unleashed dogs, especially stray dogs, were everywhere: in the street, the park, random alleys, and so on. Seeing these dogs meant running for your life and jumping on cars to survive all while praying the dog couldn't jump very high.

One day in middle school we had a half-day. That afternoon as I headed home, I walked through countless blocks and passed home after home with dogs that were chained up but barking loud as hell and looking like they'd eat you—or the next dog they'd fight.

At one point I lift my head and see a bull terrier (like the kind made famous in the Target ads) walking toward me. At the same time I look up, the dog looks up. It's as if we are thinking the same thought but for different reasons. He's like, *I'm not on a leash.* I'm like, *He's not on a leash!* Immediately after this "mirroring neurons" conversation, my default is to find the closest car. I dart off and he runs after me. I run like Carl Lewis winning the gold for both speed and long jump. But the dog puts on the speed, too, in his attempt to get me! Mercifully, I evaded the dog's attack, but not without a mental souvenir of the experience.

To this day, if I'm out and about and see a dog with no leash, I immediately think, *Car, run, safety.* According to the author of *The Body Keeps the Score*, if I give my brain new associations for unleashed dogs and experience multiple encounters where nothing negative happens in the same type of environment, it increases my default options. Session over.

CHEAT CODE NO. 14

I realized my need to partner with my wife and others' redemption stories. This insight helped me understand why tone mattered to my wife. I could see why certain embraces and specific actions of mine where reaggravating her unaddressed traumas and unhealed wounds. I could see how I could be a part of cellular redemption in her story as well as mine. This helped me apologize for the many times I put her in a position where I expected her to dig out of holes she didn't know she was in. This taught me to ask godly requests of her that were fair and relationally healthy while not being unreasonable. It allowed me to remove her from the throne where her responses affected my disposition and to let her be the perfectly imperfect human she is, not believing she needed fixing for our marriage to thrive.

> **We realized God made the body to thrive with associations of hope.**

This transferred to my kids, friends, and family. I write this as it is still in process, but I now have eyes to understand. Starting with my wife and me, we realized God made the body to either thrive with associations of hope or be destroyed with associations of toxicity. He also made the body in such an intricate way that it could be regenerated and upgraded to a state of health that has never been seen. It gave us both real joy and hope.

FUTURE CHEAT CODE

I will explore this later in the chapter, but "finding your redemption language" and understanding those you are in relationship with is huge. Having grown up as the youngest of three kids and experiencing so many traumas in my family of origin, I felt the anger of not being heard but didn't have words to describe it. I would tell my wife I wasn't being heard, and she would look at me as if she wanted to say, "How, Sway? You are the man; you're taller, louder, and more imposing."

But for me, being heard was not about any of those things. It was about being attended to; my brain and body needed new associations with attention. I was able to vocalize clearly the distress of the past, the wounds it created, and the ways new associations could take place to bring healing.

BLACKNESS REDEFINED

I believe people, especially my people, need new associations for healing when it comes to relationships—whether they want to admit it or not. Many of us are walking wounded because of how we were talked to and shamed as kids in the name of tough love. Explaining the negativity of the world to my kids will produce a different lifelong outcome than practicing toxic behaviors on them. I tell my daughter about how the world will treat her because we live in a "non-ideal world," but I don't give her practice sessions on what it's like to be bullied and receive verbal abuse. In many ways, whiteness has been the progenitor of Black folks' trauma, but I want to pass on to you these words Don Furious gave to me: "You don't have to continue to live out someone's unhealth in your life anymore."

> Whiteness may have a narrative for you, but you can actually write another one.

As Frantz Fanon says, the white man can never give the Black person their full identity. You can heal from the traumas, but who you are is not about what they stole from you. It is about who you were made to be. They cannot answer that question.

Only God, our Creator, has the answer to this question.

Don went on to say, "Whiteness may have a narrative for you, but you can actually write another one." I believed then and I am living proof now that doing the work of writing a new narrative is liberating and redemptive. Black folks, we need to write an original story for our people as it pertains to the health of our entire beings. We need to give our spouses, children, friends, and families new associations to help heal traumas at the cellular level. God gives us the tools to do so, and they are no longer hidden. Trauma's darkness doesn't have to be a part of our culture and music anymore. You have permission to write a new narrative.

If . . . (A Spoken Word)

What would it look like if a people were
    really *healed?*
I mean really *healed*
They profited off of us selling trauma stories to
    each *other*
We called it music and *culture*

Is it not sad that unprocessed pain

Was the therapy of a community and we called it
Blues, hip-hop, R+B, because legally we had
no other way to *mourn?*

But what if we didn't accept that lucrative offer to
create, distribute, disturb, and distress as the
only way out of a damaging providence, *ha-ha*

Are you telling me today—2019 the only way to
triumph is by manufacturing and packaging
torment?

Are you telling me that unhealth is the highest
good bestowed upon us by the *Creator?*

F**k that

The times have *changed*

He changed *them*

We can *conquest*

Give people healthful, healing hope without toxic
masculinity, objectification and accepting these
psychological and material places of *inferiority.*

There is a new breed of Blackness that creates
prevailing narratives, song, fashion,
and civilization

While reigning, with trauma not playing the lead in
our scripts but a small footnote in *defeat.*

CHAPTER 11

INEXHAUSTIBLE WATER

No repentance . . . no remission.

There I was in the bottom of Cape Coast Castle in Ghana. I couldn't breathe, and sweat was pouring from my body, soaking all my clothes. We were shooting a documentary about what my West African ancestors went through. We saw slave castles in southern Ghana, Elmina, and Cape Coast as well as the northern slave markets.

This experience opened my eyes to what I needed to heal from. I didn't need to recover from just my trauma and wounds; I needed to somehow embrace theirs to put mine into perspective. I needed a viewpoint to see how mighty a legacy God gave me and others from the African diaspora.

As I took this journey across Ghana, I realized there should not be an African American face alive in the Americas. The terror of the five-hundred-mile journey—

barefoot—from the northern border to the southern caves and the additional terror of the sardine-packed boats of the Middle Passage, the insanity that drove many people to death . . . it was eye-opening. Yet many survived these terrors. This was an act of the divine in our bodies. Other ethnic groups became extinct when subjected to similar situations.

I learned that part of my healing was seeing I had accepted the label of inferiority placed on me by society and life, and this did not match the gifts and strength God gave my people. I needed to mourn this and change my ways. *Anumasa* is the Ghanaian word for "inexhaustible water." It means nothing in creation can exhaust, put out, stifle, or stop the natural rushing waters God placed in nature as well as his people. When I heard this word and grew to understand it along with the horrendous story we endured, I saw for the first time that I am from a people who have survived the world's (dare I say Satan's) countless attempts to exhaust us. It has not happened, and it will not happen.

BLACKNESS REDEFINED

There comes a time where one needs to understand history and the failed attempts throughout centuries to repress your people and *see*. To see, just like Elisha asked the Lord to open the eyes of his servant so he could know they were surrounded by horses and chariots of fire (2 Kings 6:17). To see that God is with you and your people. He has been for centuries, and your wrestling is not against flesh and blood.

Once we realize our battle is predominantly mental, emotional, and spiritual, then we are able to equip ourselves in ways best suited to address the challenge confronting us. Tiger Woods did not take mini-putt clubs to the Masters Tournament, nor did Serena Williams bring ping-pong paddles to the French Open. In order to compete at the highest levels, they had to know the games they were expected to play and come equipped with the proper gear.

And how does this relate to our current journey? To paraphrase Carter G. Woodson in *The Mis-Education of the Negro*: the biggest opposition to the Black man is not the white man but the Black man who has been indoctrinated in the ways of whiteness. Whiteness can be understood from Woodson's perspective as believing the narrative of having to advance in the educational system, assimilate into the culture, and follow the vocational track laid out for you by the white majority culture in order to get ahead, even at the expense of the story, gifts, and Blackness given to you by God.

> **No longer will I apologize and give prefaces for who I am as a person because it scares someone.**

Something changed in me that day at Cape Coast, and it needs to change in all of us as Black folks. We need to be the lions God fashioned us to be. Yes, we were terrorized, and a good bit still happens today. However, our people didn't survive so that we could wallow in fear. We must seize what they could not.

No longer will I apologize and give prefaces for who I am as a person because it scares someone. The only fear one should have is that of not reaching their full potential. Someone else's fear of you succeeding should not be your barrier. I had to mourn the wounds I had accepted under the guise of humility—a traumatic identity of less-than in society. I took the position of fear and called it patience, the place of inferiority and called it trusting God, all because of a legacy of terror and propaganda. We can trust God to provide as our fullest selves just as much as we tried to be less-than and fall under the radar. Frantz Fanon advises that the Black man should not look to the white man for his measure of success but should ask the question, "Who am I?" Not basing it on what he has taken from you, but on knowing who you are and what you are worth . . . as your ceiling is higher than the cap they will put on you.

CHEAT CODE NO. 15

Our people are a mighty group on whom God bestowed a divine strength that cannot be extinguished—*anumasa*. Remember Isaiah 40? "He gives strength to the weary and increases the power of the weak" (Isaiah 40:29 NIV). Understanding our history should not make us mad at whiteness. It should make us proud and more confident of our divine attributes, which cannot be taken from us because they are God-given. Whiteness can't give you what God has declared for you to have, and it certainly can't take it away. Whiteness certainly has tried for centuries to take it away, but it will not prevail.

It is a glorious experience to see with my own eyes what we went through and to read the neurological studies of how this should have killed the brain, yet we continue to thrive as a people despite the countless attempts to stifle our "water." To know we are divinely mighty and see it with no tools is the cheat code. *We. Are. The. Cheat. Code.*

> **You have permission to live in the divine wind of God and not give away your dignity or squelch your humanity.**

In the prophetic words of Jay-Z, "We are culture . . . yet we continue to give it away." There has yet to be repentance and a tangible restorative plan addressing the sins of the American and European past. If that repentance and restorative plan ever takes shape, you will see a blessing on humanity never seen on this soil. However, even if it never happens, you have permission to live in the divine wind of God and not give away your dignity or squelch your humanity. You are an image-bearer of the almighty God, which means your value is inherent. It is not conditional. It does not need to be proved or earned for the benefit of those who do not value you as a person. You are a child of God (Romans 8:14).

We Are (A Spoken Word)

We *are*
Divine
Destined
Determined
We *are*
A *force*
Unbreakable
Unchangeable
Fortified
Infinitely endowed with an identity
That flows like the *Niagara*
Unreachable like Mount *Everest*
Deeper than the unknown ocean *floor*
We are more than the boats that brought *us*
The marches of *freedom*
The *assassinations*
The *albums*
The *fashion*
The objectification and imposed *sexualization*
The gold chains as our way of *expression*
More than the repressed feelings through *violence*
We are what has yet to be *seen*
We are defined by that which is *higher*
Not that which was taken from us
We *are* . . .

CHAPTER 12

REMOVIN' CHAINS

Partnering does not mean carrying.

This entry is one of the sweetest ones to write. I recently sat down with Don Furious to talk about life. As we got into our usual rhythm, he dropped this on me: "Partnering does not mean carrying the weight of healing. Your spouse and relationships can bring to the surface the things that need to be healed, but only God can carry the weight of that responsibility to repair."

This was revolutionary for the entire construct of who I am as a person. It was like life flashed before my eyes—the countless girlfriends and friends I'd cut off, substitute families I'd had, why I went abroad so much, playing basketball in college and overseas, all the erroneous conversations with my wife. It all became clear. I was subconsciously asking people to fill a void I did not know existed.

I came home and told my wife I wanted her to be free from deficit love. It was clear that most people love and are loved from a deficit mentality. What does that mean? It means life in alignment with Satan creates scarcities in critical areas of our lives that get buried deep in our psychology, cells, and subconscious. Because we have not named the pain, our bodies respond with expectations of others to an extreme that leaves the other party baffled. These expectations are so high they can never be met.

I had to learn what I would call my "healing language," speaking to others in a way that infuses health into my being to dissolve a traumatic past. I will get into this in the last chapter.

BLACKNESS REDEFINED

So then I had to learn the true meaning of health. I had to learn to name the pain, grieve the pain, and have the humility to admit that people and situations could hurt me. I had to ask my wife and others to walk next to me instead of carrying me. Walking side by side with someone means ultimately letting Yeshua carry us in the process. Most think their spouses, roommates, friends, bosses, coworkers, and relationships are supposed to fill voids and carry the weight of healing us, but only Yeshua has the power to

> **Walking side by side with someone means ultimately letting Yeshua carry us in the process.**

carry us. We are tasked with walking alongside each other in the valley, but God's presence gives us strength.

I recently watched a 1971 interview with Nikki Giovanni and James Baldwin on YouTube. I watched with intoxicating anticipation, and they didn't let me down. I was enthralled by Giovanni's healthy obsession with the belief that Black women deserve the best from Black men. She said, "It is not right for the Black man to go out and jive, lie, and put on a face for the white man, and then the one who loves you the most gets the least. No, put on that same face for me." I believe she is making the best point through philosophy and sarcasm. I understood her words as this: Don't smile and lie to him to make him think you like him, then come home and pour out your wrath on the Black woman in the name of provision. Don't attach your greatness to jiving for a paycheck. Love me, be loved, and keep your soul.

There is no badge anymore to pretend to love something you don't and to internalize the pain while your loved ones get the worst of you and the world gets the best—in the name of provision and sacrifice. I am with Giovanni; we are too extraordinary to sell our souls for a paycheck while destroying the Black woman and our families in the process, believing a paycheck at the expense of degradation and inferiority is our highest position in society.

The greatest thing my wife ever freed me from was the idea that I had to maintain a lifestyle to earn her love. She told me she wanted me, not a lifestyle. She never wanted me to stay in a place I hated for the sake of providing for my family. For too long, Black folks have traumatically kept themselves in positions of inferiority, being looked over for jobs, not respected for their work in the name of a paycheck. When my wife freed me from myself, it pushed me to ask, "Who am I?" Without this crutch to provide a particular lifestyle, I realized I was part of a breed greater than what society will ever attribute to the Black man and woman. Our spirits have been traumatized into a way of thinking that has atrophied our view of ourselves and the capabilities God has given us.

The chains of lifestyle and prestige at the expense of our souls and loved ones can't hold us. The question is, which one will we serve? I believe we as a people look to possessions and prestige as signs of progress because they were withheld from us for so long. So, to have them feels like progress when, in reality, they are a natural human right. So we celebrate natural rights of education and housing as if they were progress. We don't have holidays for breathing or wearing clothes because these are natural rights. However, due to the trauma imposed on an entire people group, we make holidays celebrating natural rights and call it progress. This is still a form of bondage, like P.O.W.s, from which we must break free. We need to get out, *immediately*. Jesus asked, "Is not life more than food, and the body more than clothing?" (Matthew 6:25). Lifestyle is not identity. You have permission for your Blackness to be free from the curse of obtaining things to prove your value.

Old Lover (A Spoken Word)

A cumbersome heaviness that we were assigned
    to *shoulder*
No one completes *you*
Only providing *aid*
But we turn that aid into a medical
Maid
Calling it *sweetheart*
Glorified caregiver with
Unconditional stipulations at *best*
Cloaked in *commitment*
Commitment, yes as long as
You are committed to my expectations
To undertake what is beyond *human capacity*
Holding hostage the health of each other in fetters
    that were meant for offenders of the *unhealthy*
That is *right*
You did offend *me*
For not knowing the decades of distress
I refused to release to you as
A viable way of escape and *restoration*
Because, I am *Blackness*
That Blackness will get you *killed*
Seeing and becoming nothing

But the Blackest box in the ground
Lowered into the bleakest box beyond
Everyone's *cognition*
What happened?
He/she refused to stand up to their *pain*
Confront the bully, you have yet to *reign*
Our sanity is contingent *on it.*

CHAPTER 13

THE CONQUERING LION

The Jesus you never knew.

There I was with my new friend Qaba in Khayelitsha, an impoverished community in Cape Town, South Africa. It was 2017 and I was on a journey with one of my mentees who wanted to learn firsthand about South Africa's history of racial injustice. With the help of a friend who does ministry in the country, we explored apartheid's aftermath. Although it's no longer the law of the land, its legacy of injustice and oppression is still evident. In Khayelitsha, one of the world's largest slums, we met Qaba, who invited us to his home for a conversation. Six hours later, we were still talking.

Qaba could not understand why I followed Jesus (Yeshua). He said this "white" Jesus has done nothing but harm our people. To his surprise, I told him he was right. He thought I was there to convert him, even dared me to try. I said, "I do not have a heaven or hell to put you in; that power belongs to God. I am here to hear from you as a human in God's image, and you're hearing from me as an image-bearer." I went on to tell him no man or woman has the power of God to turn anyone's soul, but we can share our story and if Adonai makes you a citizen of his domain through that sharing, that is on him. I told him I was there to listen and chat as a friend about life, humanity, and even "white Jesus." He smiled. And off we went.

We talked for hours about how it was impossible for Yeshua (Jesus) to be a white man—geographically, historically, sociologically. Where the Israelites started from, their exodus from Egypt, their conquest and captivity, and finally where Christ physically lived were so far from Europe it was comical to even speculate that Jesus was anything other than a person of color. Qaba conceded that point. We then talked about what people did in the name of "white Jesus"—how white Christianity used the Bible to kill in conquest, from Constantine's reign to the enslavement of Black folks in the pre- and post-colonial eras. Qaba said, "Why would I follow something that has ruined so many people's lives? Even if this Jesus is not white, whites have taken him and have confused and destroyed the majority of creation for centuries."

He had a point. It's a dilemma that has plagued Black apologists for ages—how do we credibly reconcile the racism and destruction performed in the name of Jesus with the message of a Savior who came to bring salvation to all people?

I paused for several seconds to ponder his question, before finally sensing God's permission to speak. "A chef's knife was created to do certain things for the purpose of preparing and making food. Even if someone misuses what the creator of the knife intended, it does not make the knife wrong; it makes those who misused it flawed. Even if the chef's knife is used as a murder weapon, it does not make the knife bad. The question to ask is, What was the creator's intent for that knife, to kill or make beautiful meals?"

I told Qaba no society in the history of humankind has eroded or been oppressed when the life and teachings of Christ have been fully applied without hypocrisy. Many have misused the Scriptures and Christ for power, murder, and their own gain. That is "murderers misusing the knife," but the problem is not the knife. I said, "Qaba, I am here to tell you, there is another option for the knife, to make beautiful meals. The Christ you know is false. I am sorry. I had to make that discovery too. But the real Jesus brings life, not death."

> **No society in the history of humankind has eroded or been oppressed when the life and teachings of Christ have been fully applied without hypocrisy.**

Qaba slowly nodded his head, his eyes opening wide as if the scales had been removed. He smiled and said, "What do you do for a living?"

My mentee piped up, "He's a professor!"

Qaba yelled, "You mean to tell me I have been going back and forth with a professor for six hours?" We all laughed. Then Qaba said, "*Lumkile!* You are 'the wise one' for your approach . . . *Lumkile.*" And like that, I had a new nickname.

I learned that *lumkile* (pronounced LOOM-key-lay) is a Xhosa word for "wise one." That day remains one of the sweetest, most unforced times in my life. It was one of those rare moments when I felt, *THIS is how Yeshua would've done it.*

WRAPPED IN MINORITY SKIN

I believe most people for good, bad, and delusion think Jesus is fair-skinned and at best do not think this matters to the potency of understanding how Christ related to creation day in and day out. But now I realize how wrong it is to depict and assume Christ had a skin color he didn't. Let's look at the Scriptures, as what comes next is huge revelation from on high.

The apostle Paul wrote to the Corinthian church, "For you know how generous our Lord Yeshua the Messiah was—for your sakes he impoverished himself, even though he was rich, so that he might make you rich by means of his poverty" (2 Corinthians 8:9 CJB).

Without teaching an entire class on the subject, I will say there is one question and three things making this passage the greatest reality about Yeshua. First, how did he impoverish himself? The definition of "impoverish" is to reduce to poverty and make poor. This boundless king and Conquering Lion could have wrapped himself in any skin tone, even the fair skin of the majority culture Romans, but he chose not to; he chose the minority skin tone. Yeshua wrapped himself in Jewish skin, and the Romans picked up where the Greeks left off—oppressing and disdaining the Jews.

> **Jesus did not wrap himself in the majority culture's skin, region, or class and *that matters.***

Yeshua did not choose the majority skin but that of the subjected minority. Not only did he impoverish himself in brown Jewish skin; he also chose the least-regarded region as his home: Nazareth. Not only did he choose the subjected minority skin and the least-regarded region; he also chose working-class parents who were considered less-than by both the Romans and even the higher-ranking Jews. Remember the Jewish people's low estimation of the family? "Is not this the carpenter's son?" (Matthew 13:55). If you are teaching a "white Jesus," one of privilege or simple indifference, you will never notice these vital realities.

It matters that a Savior knew every day what it meant to be subjected down to the very skin that wrapped him. It matters that a Savior knew disgrace based on the region he came out of and the class of people he came from. To depict otherwise and be indifferent to these realities is to miss the potency of Christ's life and for Qaba and others to reject a "white Jesus" who is erroneously promoted everywhere but who is a false god.

The Jesus you never knew, Yeshua, suffered in respect to all humankind and is able to run to the aid of those who call on him.

> This is why he had to become like his brothers in every respect—so that he might become a merciful and faithful *cohen gadol* [high priest] in the service of God, making a *kapparah* for the sins of the people. For since he himself suffered death when he was put to the test, he is able to help those who are being tested now. (Hebrews 2:17-18 CJB)

This Jesus knows what it means to be subjected and inferior down to his very skin tone, region, and class, to the point that it affected his approach to life every time he went out the door. *That matters.* I may never know if Jesus was exactly Black like me, but I do know he knew what it meant to be in brown skin, subjected and subjugated, a member of a class of people who were disdained by the majority culture. Jesus did not wrap himself in the majority culture's skin, region, or class and *that matters.*

I have not seen many make themselves tangibly poor like Yeshua did in order for others to be lifted up. It is natural to want to go up in class, to climb society's proverbial ladder. But only something beyond this creation will get people to go from riches to rags for the sake of others.

BREAKING THE CHAINS

As you have probably discovered, Jay-Z's and Lauryn Hill's music was a foundational soundtrack during my journey to healing and liberation. In another song from Hill's *Unplugged* album, she says, "The conquering lion shall break every chain . . . give him the victory, again and again and again."

As we journey deeper into this chapter, know this: the healing journey is never over. You never stop running the race; it is a lifelong marathon. However, joy can be found in the race, even if true never-ending joy will never be had until our citizenship is fully realized beyond this world. The race is not pain-free. There are cramps, tightness, sweat, tears, frustrations, and mental wrestling to overcome the impulse to quit. Yet, the race can be run with joy.

You may wonder, what pace is healthy? Some days you will run faster in the direction of health than others. Some days you will walk, and some days you will crawl. But we must never stop moving toward health and freedom.

We can be overly concerned with speaking in code as disciples of Yeshua, to let other faiths know we are open and not like "the other Christ followers," but my first love cannot be dialed down. In some ways it should be intoxicating. My love for my wife and how I love others are things to be envied, not ashamed of. The truth is this: if I were held hostage and someone freed me with their might and resources, I would let everyone know who rescued me. To talk in code so people don't know who did this incredible work in your life is disingenuous.

Yeshua is kind, powerful, understanding, and dynamic, but he is also the one who receives my deepest affections. He is the one who came in subjected skin and redeemed me during my darkest times. No one on this earth can claim that or has the capacity to manifest love and kindness in his ways, where they would make themselves poor for their entire life on earth so I could become rich. Yeshua is the one I love, and with his approach to love, we should be able to converse with and love anyone. I was introduced to him at ten when I was young but was told I was going to hell because I did not speak in tongues. Imagine what that does to a ten-year-old. My brain did not understand what the journey meant until I met Brian Buck, who gave me an NIV Bible to read for myself. But then I was introduced to a "white Jesus" who did not love all of me; I had to traverse freedom from that subculture as well. This is a journey, not a destination point on earth.

The Conquering Lion showed me I must have the humility to invite people onto the road of healing but not expect them to shoulder an inhumane weight only the Conquering Lion is meant to carry. They can partner, yes, but only the Conquering Lion can break the chains. I realized I put others in the position to be the Conquering Lion when only Yeshua has the power to break chains and give victory again and again and again. Motives do not remove pain. Yeshua showed me this. In this process over the last two years, I discovered what I would call my healing-redemption language, and I want to share with you how I found it and help you find out yours.

Healing and redemption are a cocktail; in different seasons, you may need various forms of practices and information. Discovering your healing language is about naming what key distressing situations (traumas) happened in your life. These are the experiences you merely "moved past" (internalized) but didn't grieve, leaving wounds that negatively impact how you see the world.

A key part of my healing-redemption journey was to name that I was emotionally orphaned by my parents, and this wound created the framework for gravitating toward family units (white or Black) who would embrace me as I sought nurturing. I had to name that I was told to edit myself as a person and in doing so lived a castrated version of who God made me to be. I needed a language spoken to me by those who would give me their best and not seek to edit me. I remember one family unit, Tom and Lessie Bryce, who loved me through college like none other.

I was set to go to Long Beach, California, for a fashion gig. The company said if I could get there, the gig was mine. There was just one problem: I had no money and so I had no way to get to California. I put this need before my community, and Tom Bryce offered me his Ford Ranger truck—not to borrow but to have. Tom was not rich—he needed that truck for work—but he gave me his best that day. I drove to Cali in the summer of 2002 and it was magical. When it came time to let go of that truck six years later, it was hard. I realize now there were very few times I received someone's best. That gesture redeemed pieces in me then that I did not have the language to describe. I didn't understand then why it mattered, but it did and still does. To know God wants to give me his best and to tell others my redemptive language is freeing. I'm also now able to understand (sometimes) that others want to give me their best but just can't, and this is not a form of abandonment. That ability is liberating! This reality *freed my soul*; it broke heavy chains of doubt in my life.

Growing up I often heard a voice in my head loudly proclaiming, "You are not worth anyone's best." With

Being my full self around others is love.

Don Furious, I was able to name and grieve that, to talk about how to express pain to others to keep from internalizing it. Chains started to break and eventually dissolve. I began to heal, certain things ceased to be triggers, and I could deal with my wife, family, and friends in the present without being triggered by the past.

I tell my community and others that my healing-redemption language is this: *the little things of your best efforts matter and being my full self around others is love.* My brain appreciates gestures such as replies to text messages, rides to and from the airport when I can easily take a rideshare, face-to-face conversations, and follow-up from loved ones on issues I've shared that are sensitive to my soul. It isn't because I need them to fill a hole but because it gives me a new association for my brain. It is life for me. These actions manifest the reality of newness in my mental framework. This language of nurturing and receiving someone's best through the small things is healing.

Another part of my healing-redemption language is people assuming the best of my motives even when my imperfect actions miss the mark. I can hear when a person assumes the worst, and I want to verbally fight. I hated physical fights in my childhood; as an adult, I hate both physical and emotional fights. I ask people to believe I am about peace and not about "those hands."

Another element of my redeeming language is the freedom to express "griefs and longings" and not be held captive by the dialogue of persuasion. (I gleaned this wisdom from a personal conversation with author Curt Thompson.) Loved ones should not have to persuade or be persuaded if there is trust in the relationship and both parties are healed. Trust precedes the conversation with those we love, and so does the healing. If we don't trust a person, they will have to convince us. This is not best, but many in the world operate this way, even with those we say we deeply "trust" and love. I have let the ones I love know that convincing me will not be a part of the relationship.

Lastly, a healed person must be liberated to live as Adonai made them to be, not as society or any Christian sect says they should. The late evangelist Tom Skinner, in his message to the Black Student Union of Augsburg University on December 8, 1971, said: "A nigga is a person who allows somebody else to define him. . . . Jesus says I have come to give you good news . . . to help you define yourself on the basis of who God says you are, not on the basis of who society says."

I am a Black man, though healed; I realize my zeal is a gift from God. Some may label me as very zealous, or a zealot, and that's fine. Jesus had a zealot in his group who was an apostle: "Simon who was called the Zealot" (Luke 6:15). Zealots believed in kingdom violence when their humanity and worship were at stake. We see Jesus practicing this reality in celebrating the Feast of Dedication in John 10:22-23 (also known as Hanukkah), which commemorates the rededication of the temple after the Maccabees, led by Judas the Hammer, rose up against their Greek Syrian oppressors. I do not believe in preemptive violence, but I do believe we must be ready for what comes our way physically or spiritually, and Jesus was not passive—far from it.

Jesus knew Peter and his other disciples rolled with a sword. He wasn't surprised by it—check the passage here:

But Yeshua said to him, "Y'hudah [Judas], are you betraying the Son of Man with a kiss?" When his followers saw what was going to happen, they said, "Lord, should we use our swords?" One of them struck at the slave of the *cohen hagadol* and cut off his right ear. But Yeshua answered, "Just let me do this," and, touching the man's ear, he healed him. (Luke 22: 48-51 CJB)

Many assume Jesus was against swords, but earlier in Luke he says, "If you don't have a sword, sell your robe to buy one" (Luke 22:36 CJB). Jesus understood the times. He also understood that we are not to live all of life by the way of the sword.

I am not campaigning for swords, but I am showing you Jesus was not naive to what it took in the days of Roman rule or what it meant to live as a kingdom citizen. Scholars are split on whether Simon Peter and Simon the Zealot are the same person, but that is not the point. The point is, Yeshua surrounded himself with zealous folks.

From age seventeen to thirty-four, I spent my Christian life in white churches being told I needed to get rid of my zeal because God couldn't use it and it "intimidated" others, only to realize that God gave me my zeal as a gift and I was letting a culture, not God, define who I was as a Black man. I was allowing my God-given zeal and prophetic edge to be edited out. Redemption of the full self means embracing all the pains and personality of who God designed you to be. Even if it comes with less material gain in this world, you are fully embraced by Adonai.

CHEAT CODE NO. 16

You find your redemption language by asking the questions of emotions. Take the questions Don Furious asked me: "What emotions come to mind when I say 'mother,' 'father,' 'siblings,' 'cousins,' 'teachers,' 'city,' and so on?" Make a list of people you know were a part of your life then and now. What are the emotions you feel in response to them and the environment? What is your birth order? What distressing situations occurred in your life to shape the way you see the world? What does your brain default to when it comes to certain critical areas of life, especially relationships with others (friends, coworkers, parents)? If joy is not the emotion that comes forth, then healing and a redemptive language are needed.

BLACKNESS REDEFINED

The day my wife, friends, and family ceased to offend me was the day I was able to love and be loved by them. Blackness in so many ways is about "not letting sh*t slide." Be it Snoop saying, "We can handle this like some gentlemen, or we can get into some gangsta sh*t" ("U Betta

Recognize," 1994) to the *Boyz n the Hood* scene where Ricky and Doughboy's refusal to "let it slide" results in a shooting. I could go on. There's O-Dog's "You feel sorry for *who*?" in *Menace II Society* just before he kills a couple who insulted him, or the scene in *Above the Rim* when Tupac's character, Birdie, kills Flip with a razor because he can't let things slide. The refusal to let things slide is a common depiction in many Black films in recent history. In life, we respond as if every imperfect act or word is about us, but it is not. Most times, someone else's actions are about their unprocessed trauma, and we react from our own unhealed wounds.

When you take yourself out of the center of others' imperfect actions toward you, you cease to be offended. When you can name your pain and grieve with real tears, you cease to be offended. When you can humbly talk about the things you long to do but wonder if they will come about without judgment, freedom comes and offense dissolves. The Conquering Lion heals our brokenness and shame. Internalized battles wage war in your body and your neurological system and keep you a prisoner of your pain.

This book is about navigating the Black experience in America. Much can be said about the racism and trauma experienced by Native Americans, Asians, and Latinos in this country, but as you've noticed, I'm limiting it to Black people here.

Black folks, Africans of the diaspora, have experienced an extreme level of darkness on American soil.

From explicit laws making it illegal for us to process our humanity to societal constructs of terror keeping us from voting and progressing in education or building a financial legacy, Black folks have dealt with numerous brands of oppression for over four hundred years now.

However, in the kingdom of Yeshua, there are two types of darkness. One is the kind found in the conversation Yeshua has with Peter about feeding his sheep. This comes after Peter wept bitterly because he denied Christ three times. The darkness Peter saw in himself was the darkness and void of his past, filled with trauma—mind, body, and soul—from which the same reality will come if he defines himself by the denial (John 21:14-17). Living in the regrets of your past is pleasing to Satan.

But there is another darkness—a darkness of hope, the unseen. This darkness is what the world is created from. "In the beginning, God created the heavens and the earth . . . and darkness was over the face of the deep" (Genesis 1:1-2). It was a darkness bustling with hope, a canvas of what had yet to be discovered that produced—the beautiful Eden then, and the world we know now. The darkness of an unknown hope is reassuring because God promises to build something new we

> **The darkness of an unknown hope is reassuring because God promises to build something new we have yet to see.**

have yet to see. We see this promise in both Genesis and John 1, as we learn of the Spirit of God hovering over the void and proclaiming, "Let there be light."

Both kinds of darkness are real, but the older darkness has proven itself to be imprisonments of pain, whereas this new darkness, a darkness of hope, is based on the unseen because it has not happened yet. So yes, when you say, "I don't know this new way," smile and walk with God because he is about to show you your Eden. *It is out of darkness* that your new world will come.

CHEAT CODE NO. 17

My new Blackness had to face the darkness of my past— the past that "you don't talk about" in Black communities. In facing my past darkness, I was able to heal from it. This allowed me to turn my face toward the new darkness: a darkness of the unknown, a darkness of hope. Black folks, may we be people who process our past darkness to embrace a new one of hope. May we be people of tangible hope. May we be people who do the work as we are led by the Conquering Lion who breaks every chain.

Nothing Like . . . (A Spoken Word)

There is nothing like *penitentiary*
Not the one where you are convicted of
Said *crime*
But the one where you are convicted

And sentenced to a life walled *in*

Walled in by traumas enacted upon you

Because health was not in the legacy

Of your *DNA*

So, your parents internalize to

Manifest pain that develops practices

Of the same internalization and

Pain *manifestations*

There is nothing like walking free in the cool in the
day but freely being imprisoned by pains you
feel are

Abnormal but lack the dialogue and language,
foreign it feels, to convey

The reality of where you *are.*

There is nothing like *prison*

Prison of the mind and body while

Many see an external strength

That feels like the biggest lie of *peace*

All you feel is *turmoil*

Every day you wake up to the emotional smell of
hopelessness

The mental stench of guards who are looking for a
reason to degrade you into nothing lingers in
your *head*

The bleak light of hope contrasts with the

Psychological closeness of shadows and cement and
routine of

You not being worthy of life and a *chance*

The cerebral defeat of walking a routine

Line with others who are in the same prison
becomes normal and somewhat natural
because prison has settled itself into your body
and endurance is the air you breathe as your
dreams of relief will come when God calls
you *homeward*

There is nothing like *freedom*

When you hear that your term has been reduced
from life to *days*

You think, can I do life outside this *prison?*

You are told by those on the outside that

You are made for more than this prison you have
known for most of *life*

Having to trust no one and be a friend unto
yourself is *over.*

There is nothing like hearing the bars open and
knowing you will never walk the line of
routine toward the yard trading jokes about
mental *penitentiary*

There is nothing like hearing that gate close behind
you and you walking toward an unknown of
newness where the sun's shine is almost
blinding because your mental and emotional
eyes adjusted to the *darkness.*

There is nothing like *freedom*

CONCLUSION

AWAKEN US AND
THE ONE PERCENT

What do you call a dream deferred? . . . Does it explode?

LANGSTON HUGHES, "HARLEM"

I am not God (goes without saying, I know), so I cannot see it all. I can't see who does and does not work on behalf of Black life. But history says this: very few people across global ethnic lines nail themselves to the daily plight of Black life as it pertains to our human rights. Human rights and civil rights are not the same. I am endowed with rights as a human because of the life given to me by God. Civil rights are a matter of societal constructions and contracts, and society is developed under law. Civil rights do not determine our humanity and the God-given rights we have. If you respond to the violation of our humanity only when the grossest tragedy occurs in civil sectors, then you have a blind spot of privilege no rhetoric will help you see. You are part of the problem.

....

Only the willfully ignorant person believes evil will one day die off and evolve out of itself into good. This ignorance believes the same evil is restricted to isolated occurrences despite its tentacles extending from a metastasized history of vile beliefs and practices. To echo both Billie and Kanye, the strange fruit and blood on the leaves still cry out.

Remember the one percent statistic I shared earlier about free Black men who are alive with the resources, tools, health, community, education, and presence to do something redemptive? I want to give you an illustration of how rare this is.

At the time of writing this book my wife and I decided to buy a home. I'd rather buy acres and build than buy a fast-food-construction home on a ten-thousand-square-foot lot, so we compromised on 1.26 acres. The process to find this type of home in Atlanta was not easy. We went on real-estate apps and began to add filter after filter: "buying a home," "4 bed, 3+ bath," "2500+ sq. ft." Everything was plentiful until we put in "1+ acre." Suddenly the available houses went from three hundred down to five. We were stunned at the scarcity. Back to the stat.

Reader, I charge you to understand how rare and scarce Black men are—just like my wife and me looking for that specific home. When you ask the Black male, given this country's history of exclusion and oppression, to grow up in a broken home and broken community, make it through the gauntlet of violence with no father figure, graduate high school, go to college, not get addicted to drugs, not objectify women, understand money and wealth-building, appreciate their skin color, honorably represent all Black people, get married, have kids, raise them, understand corporate America, smile, and pursue Christ and his kingdom—all with no manual—it is insane. Many people view these expected achievements as par for the course, but the truth is these milestones are not experienced by an abundance of Black men. Anthropological social evolution without a manual does not exist. The expectation that young Black males should through sheer character and willpower overcome all the disadvantages American society bestows on them even before birth and somehow thrive is unrealistic and delusional.

My older brother said this to me while I was writing this book and sharing these stats:

A friend of mine and teammate at Cass Tech . . . Mario Washington was brutally murdered while in high school. . . . He wasn't a thug. . . . He wasn't a bad student. . . . He was working at Little Caesar's when a robbery went wrong . . . dead at sixteen years.

Why wasn't that me, God, why wasn't that my fate? I'm sure he had people praying for him too. Knowing that God for some reason chose *you* for this moment is a heavy weight and responsibility to own and walk under.

Black men, especially of this one percent, need to be affirmed. The very fact of their survival, and God's preservation of them, says so. We are in a fight, a supernatural fight we were dropped into that started long before us, yet we're still expected to make up the deficit and rise to the challenge. Be perfect in corporate America, at church, at traffic stops, with your wife and kids, shed and redefine stereotypes you had nothing to do with while internalizing the expression and weight of it all. If you look at the census of African Americans and also Black males, you'll see our numbers are dwindling.

> There is more to aspire to and be inspired by, beyond focusing on what we were robbed of.

This book cannot be the conclusive answer to all our problems. I would be arrogant and delusional to think I could write such a work.

The hope of this book is inspiration and aspiration. I believe, for people of color, there is more to aspire to and be inspired by, beyond focusing on what we were robbed of. I hope this book presses the reader to believe health is the option of normal. I hope this book pushes Black folks into an awareness that what has been called Blackness in a traditional sense is not God's best for us. I wish I could say I have more answers than questions after taking this journey, but I don't. I don't have answers for a person who reads this and acknowledges their need to pursue health but is in a toxic home environment. I don't have answers for families who know only one way of relating to each other (a poisonous way) and think seeking mental, emotional, and spiritual health means "something is wrong with you." I don't have answers for our traumatized norm.

I would argue that even if Black people did have the same educational and financial opportunities in this country as whites, the march to have the emotional freedom void of backlash is far from over. Because of centuries' worth of steeped prejudice and stereotypes embedded into the culture in its fearful depiction of us, many don't realize it is a march, so many have yet to even start. The first *Birth of a Nation* was a 1915 movie depicting the Ku Klux Klan as crusading heroes. This unapologetically racist film winning the equivalent of an Academy Award is proof of a reality still being played out in how Black people are depicted through the media and police reports.

In 2016 a laundry detergent brand from China caused a big WTF when it released a television commercial many considered racist. In the ad, a Chinese woman and a Black man flirt a bit before the woman forcibly sticks a detergent pod into the man's mouth and stuffs him into a washing machine. When the man emerges from the machine, he has been magically transformed (washed?) into a clean-cut Chinese man. The devaluing of Black humanity is real.

But despite these somewhat overwhelming stats and scandals, there is a new morning. Black people have begun to see the reality of racial trauma in our community. Many people are now realizing we cannot process and survive this stuff on our own. This is one reason why I and my team members at Red Revolution Ministries (iamredrev.com) are making ourselves available to answer your questions and continue the conversation. The generational importance of this healing work is too great to let your journey conclude with these pages. Please do not hesitate to reach out to us.

God will not have the door locked if you attempt to walk into the room of health.

> **God will not have the door locked if you attempt to walk into the room of health.**

What I am talking about is not something we have seen but a new Blackness—a collaboration requiring all of us to bring resources, videos, films, plays, discussions, music, sermons, startup companies, and so on to build a new community-based understanding of health. What I've shared in this book is something I believe can happen only with God awakening a people who have known only one way to live life. For me, this way of living—internalizing my emotions and not recognizing God's love and power in me—left me battling onslaughts of depression and despair. And it is destroying the joy of many others right now. My hope is that God will awaken us all to the knowledge that emotional health is not something for the privileged of this world but a precious gift for all of his beloved creation.

God, awaken us all to your dream that does not need to be deferred anymore.

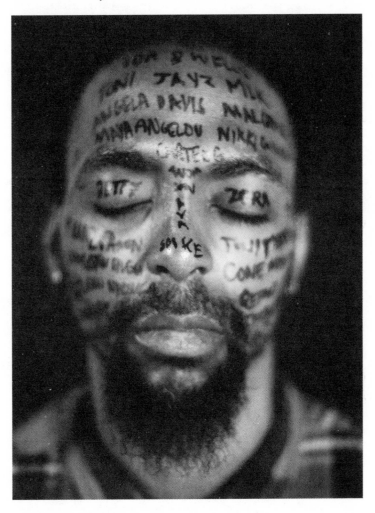

APPENDIX

BONUS CHEAT CODES

Redefining Blackness Through Films

s a poet and filmmaker, I like reading between the lines of art to figure out the layered meanings. I especially find value in analyzing great movies. With the bonus cheat codes below, I invite you to check out this collection of some of my favorite classic (and soon-to-be-classic) films. Watch them with friends, and then use my random reflections on the films as talking points for your group discussions.

COMING TO AMERICA (1988)

"They have the golden arches; we have the golden arcs. They have the Big Mac; we have the Big Mc."

This funny dialogue is the reality of what Black men and women have seen as a success, copying the methods of whiteness to make it.

SCHOOL DAZE (1988)

The clash between the dark-skinned Blacks (jigaboos) and light-skinned Blacks (wannabes) explores the trauma of colorism in the Black community. Light-skinned Blacks are often seen as not being Black enough, but society rewards them for this, allowing them to move ahead. This tension explored in the movie is present in our community. It's a false standard of Blackness and it's still an issue to this day (*to dis day*). We have been pitted against each other for survival. We must succeed together or die together, but we must no longer see one another as the enemy.

DO THE RIGHT THING (1989)

In a riot outside Sal's pizzeria, Spike Lee's character throws a trashcan through the window yelling, "*Radio!*"

The police kill Radio Raheem through a chokehold, despite the crowd's pleas for them to let him go. The onlookers want to let out their pain. They cannot take out their pain on the white police officers, so they take it out on Sal, who is also white. Sal has insurance. He will be okay. "Riot is the voice of the unheard."

GLORY (1989)

Denzel's character gets whipped, and a tear rolls down his cheek. "All he wanted was some boots."

It isn't merely the whip but the compounded issue that he isn't deserving of boots and is whipped for trying to live like a human while preparing for war in a country that does not see him as equal.

BOYZ N THE HOOD (1991)

Tre is punching the air, swinging in frustration and hysteria. He knows he can't go out in the streets, and this is his way of releasing the trauma of his friend dying. He represents our frustration of being stuck with no answers or alternatives to internalizing. When we get to that point, all we are left with is swinging in the air.

NEW JACK CITY (1991)

"This is bigger than Nino Brown."

Wesley Snipe's character says this while he is on the witness stand ranting about how he is the victim and had no choice but to sell drugs. This scene shows the reality of what Black men feel; growing up in the hood is not their ideal situation and their options are limited. The hypocrisy of government selling drugs and funding Colombian contra as long as they have the rules and "utilitarian" justification on their side is what Nino explores. So, a Nino Brown character and real-life drug dealers don't see the difference between themselves and the government when it comes to morals. Except one can make and enforce the rules in their favor even when they break them.

MALCOLM X (1992)

"You said you were not selling me no two-bit hustle."

Denzel as Malcolm X realizes the Nation of Islam is being hypocritical by allowing Elijah Mohammed to preach purity and faithfulness while he fathers many illegitimate children behind closed doors. The trauma of realizing deception in a trusted religious community is brutal. He has given his life and a ton of his best years to a lie.

MENACE II SOCIETY (1993)

O-Dog is in the grocery store, and his character overreacts to a comment about his mother. Though this is a scene from a movie, the aggression is real. Cats got smoked over shoes and comments like these. Why? It's the shooter's way of using a gun to let out their aggression.

ABOVE THE RIM (1994)

Tom Shepherd, played by Leon, is not able to deal with the trauma of losing his friend. As a result, he forfeits his ability to go to college and eventually go pro. This story is par for the course in a ton of Black communities.

FRESH (1994)

In the final scene where the kid shows up to play chess and starts sobbing, this is indicative of what many of us had to go through. We have shouldered a weight and responsibility sooner than our emotions were ready to handle, and we just break.

FRIDAY (1995)

"I have mind control over Deebo. . . ."

Smokey, Chris Tucker's character, along with others is terrorized by the neighborhood bully, Deebo. They want to fight and defeat Deebo but do not have the power to do so. All they can do is internalize and just take what Deebo does to them. There is no one to talk to.

FRUITVALE STATION (2013)

"You shot me. . . . You shot me in the back, bro?"

Oscar Grant III is asking this question in confusion, as he realizes what should not have happened *happened*. His life slowly fades from his body and his encounter with the police does not end the way he imagined. He is not a threat, already lying on the ground helpless. Yet he is fatally shot in the back. The questions depicted in the film are a bigger narrative of what I feel Blacks ask of white America in general: You're treating us like *this*? Unarmed and complying, and still. . . . The confusion in the tone played out by Michael B. Jordan is a constant confusion I have. Why are you so skittish of a people group that makes up less than 14 percent of America, and the male population less than that?

13TH (2016)

"So many aspects of the old Jim Crow are suddenly legal again once you've been branded a felon." (Comment by Michelle Alexander.)

This brilliant documentary by Ava DuVernay analyzes how America traded one slave force for another by privatizing prisons and filling them disproportionately with Black people. If prisons are supposed to be for reform yet businesses can now get contract agreements with prisons and sue them when they don't fulfill the terms, how can reform be genuinely reached? Let this sink in: some prisons are publicly traded companies.

GET OUT (2017)

"I find navigating society as a Black man quite riveting."

Get Out stirred the cinema and Black social media world with its biting commentary on what whites really think of Black folks. We have the bodies, but white folks have the brains. This led to now and forever the idea of Black folks being in "the sunken place." In the movie it means a Black person is stolen and hijacked; today it speaks of a Black person who has a whitewashed mind and, dare I say, a "cooning" mentality. Something happened where the real Black soul of the person is not there and is trying to get out. Carter G. Woodson would call it "the mis-education of the negro" while Frantz Fanon would call it "black skin, white mask."

BLACK PANTHER (2018)

"Aren't you the king? . . . So doesn't that mean all people are your people?"

"I am not king of all people. . . . I am king of Wakanda."

Black Panther is polarizing on many levels. This dialogue between Killmonger and T'Challa for me sums up the entire movie and the reality that all Black folks do not see life the same and possibly never will. Killmonger is the son, cousin, and prince abandoned at a young age. He is left to fend for himself, though the king of Wakanda knows he is out there. As he gets older and understands what his people in Oakland need, what his deceased dad was trying to accomplish, he does not look with favor on the Wakandan Empire and its people. He feels disdain for their selfishness. The tension of "help the collective community" versus "fend for your subcultural kin" plagues us even today.

NOTES

PREFACE: BEYOND OUR "FAMILY FEUD"

4   *Take the percentage:* Justin Wolfers and David Leonhardt, "1.5 Million Missing Black Men," *The New York Times*, April 20, 2015, www.ny times.com/interactive/2015/04/20/upshot/missing-black-men.html.

5   *Of those 15.7 million:* Sophia Kerby, "The Top 10 Most Startling Facts About People of Color and Criminal Justice in the United States," Center for American Progress, March 13, 2012, www.american progress.org/issues/race/news/2012/03/13/11351/the-top-10-most -startling-facts-about-people-of-color-and-criminal-justice-in-the -united-states/.

    Until the last quarter: Richard Rothstein, *The Color of Law: A Forgotten History of How Our Government Segregated America* (New York: Liveright, 2017), 5-6.

16   *That the Negro American:* Daniel Patrick Moynihan, *The Negro Family: The Case for National Action* (Washington, DC: US Department of Labor, 1965).

    For this, most of all: Lyndon B. Johnson, "To Fulfill These Rights" (commencement address, Howard University, Washington, DC, June 4, 1965).

INTRODUCTION: EAGLE'S WINGS

29   *You don't want me to see:* Jay-Z, "Jay-Z and Dean Baquet: On Therapy, Politics, Marriage, the State of Rap and Being a Black Man in Trump's America," Dean Baquet, *The New York Times Style Magazine*, November 27, 2017, www.nytimes.com/interactive/2017/11/29 /t-magazine/jay-z-dean-baquet-interview.html.

1. THE MASQUERADE

38   *With young girls:* Sowande' M. Mustakeem, *Slavery at Sea: Terror, Sex, and Sickness in the Middle Passage* (Champaign: University of Illinois Press, 2016), 66-67.

41   *Pop-culture icon Charlemagne:* Charlamagne Tha God, *Shook One: Anxiety Playing Tricks on Me* (New York: Atria Books, 2018).

....

41 *For additional reading*: Bessel van der Kolk, *The Body Keeps the Score: Brain, Mind, and Body in the Healing of Trauma* (New York: Penguin, 2014); Curt Thompson, *The Soul of Shame: Retelling the Stories We Believe About Ourselves* (Downers Grove, IL: InterVarsity Press, 2015); W. E. B. Du Bois, *The Souls of Black Folk* (Mineola, NY: Dover Publications, [1903] 2016).

2. HELPLESS HOPE

49 *Deborah Gray White argues*: Sowande' M. Mustakeem, *Slavery at Sea: Terror, Sex, and Sickness in the Middle Passage* (Champaign: University of Illinois Press, 2016), 108-9.

6. THE MASTERMIND

88 *Audiobook recommended by Don Furious*: Bessel van der Kolk, *The Body Keeps the Score: Brain, Mind, and Body in the Healing of Trauma* (New York: Penguin, 2014).

The book contextualized research: Curt Thompson, *The Soul of Shame: Retelling the Stories We Believe About Ourselves* (Downers Grove, IL: InterVarsity Press, 2015); Curt Thompson, *Anatomy of the Soul: Surprising Connections Between Neuroscience and Spiritual Practices That Can Transform Your Life and Relationships* (Carol Stream, IL: Tyndale House Publishers, 2010); Caroline Leaf, *Switch on Your Brain: The Key to Peak Happiness, Thinking, and Health* (Grand Rapids, MI: Baker, 2013).

89 *It is possible to train*: van der Kolk, *The Body Keeps the Score*.

At the cellular level: Leaf, *Switch on Your Brain*.

91 *When someone is naked*: David Fohrman, *The Beast That Crouches at the Door* (Baltimore: HFBS Publishing, 2007), 27.

7. WHERE IS MY CAR?

101 *Internalization of trauma reaching*: Caroline Leaf, "How to Recover from Trauma and Deal with the Hard Stuff in Life," drleaf.com, July 24, 2019, https://drleaf.com/blogs/news/how-to-recover-from-trauma-and-deal-with-the-hard-stuff-in-life.

8. NEW RULES, NEW LOVE

108 *It appears, by experience*: John Woolman, *Some Considerations on the Keeping of Negroes* (Philadelphia, 1754), 15.

109   *We need to stop looking*: Frantz Fanon, *Black Skin, White Masks* (New York: Grove Press, 1952).

10. A NEW NARRATIVE

120   *The healing power*: Bessel van der Kolk, *The Body Keeps the Score: Brain, Mind, and Body in the Healing of Trauma* (New York: Penguin, 2014).

121   *Mirroring neurons conversation*: van der Kolk, *Body Keeps the Score*, 58-60.

If I give my brain: van der Kolk, *Body Keeps the Score*.

124   *the white man can never*: Frantz Fanon, *Black Skin, White Masks* (New York: Grove Press, 1952).

11. INEXHAUSTIBLE WATER

128   *The biggest opposition*: Carter G. Woodson, *The Mis-Education of the Negro* (Mineola, NY: Dover Publications, [1933] 2005), 15.

130   *We are culture*: Jay-Z, "Jay-Z - Rap Radar Podcast (Part 1)," Sept. 6, 2017, *Rap Radar Podcast*, YouTube video, youtu.be/-9vNRZ0s6XM.

12. REMOVIN' CHAINS

134   *It is not right*: Nikki Giovanni, "James Baldwin and Nikki Giovanni, a Conversation [Full]," recorded November 1971, London, for *Soul!* youtu.be/eZmBy7C9gHQ.

13.THE CONQUERING LION

149   *A nigga is a person*: Tom Skinner, "Tom Skinner, Opening Convocation (1971)," Opening Convocation, Augsburg University, December 8, 1971, www.youtube.com/watch?v=hJrivZv5mRg.

MORE RESOURCES FROM
A. D. THOMASON

I AM RED REV is the ministry platform of A. D. "Lumkile" Thomason. For more information about A. D. and the issues covered in this book, visit iamredrev.com. To see A. D. recite the spoken-word poetry featured in these pages, check out permissiontobeblack.com.